Living the Country Dream

STORIES FROM Harrowsmith CountryLife

Living the Country Dream

STORIES FROM Harrowsmith CountryLife

Compiled by Tom Cruickshank

FIREFLY BOOKS

A FIREFLY BOOK

Published by Firefly Books Ltd. 2007

FIRST PRINTING

Publisher Cataloging-in-Publication Data (U.S.)
Living the country dream : stories from Harrowsmith Country Life / compiled by Tom Cruickshank.
[256] p. : col. ill., col. photos. ; cm.
Includes index.
Selected articles from *Harrowsmith Country Life*. Topics include lifestyle, do-it-yourself projects, sustainable living, gardening, livestock and recipes.
ISBN-13: 978-1-55407-272-9 (pbk.)
ISBN-10: 1-55407-272-7 (pbk.)
ISBN-13: 978-1-55407-271-2 (bound)
ISBN-10: 1-55407-271-9 (bound)
1. Country life – Periodicals – Canada.
2. Gardening – Periodicals – Canada.
3. Do-it-yourself work. I. Cruickshank, Tom.
II. Harrowsmith country life
(North York, Ont.). III. Title.
630.971/05 dc22   S522.C2H37 2007

Library and Archives Canada Cataloguing in Publication
Living the country dream : stories from Harrowsmith country life / compiled by Tom Cruickshank.
Includes index.
ISBN-13: 978-1-55407-272-9 (pbk.)
ISBN-10: 1-55407-272-7 (pbk.)
ISBN-13: 978-1-55407-271-2 (bound)
ISBN-10: 1-55407-271-9 (bound)
1. Country life. 2. Country life—Canada. 3. Gardening.
4. Do-it-yourself work. 5. Cookery.
I. Cruickshank, Tom, 1954–
II. Title: Harrowsmith country life.
S521.L59 2007   630   C2007-900832-1

Published in the United States by
Firefly Books (U.S.) Inc.
P.O. Box 1338, Ellicott Station
Buffalo, New York 14205

Published in Canada by
Firefly Books Ltd.
66 Leek Crescent
Richmond Hill, Ontario L4B 1H1

Cover and interior design: Gareth Lind / LINDdesign

Editorial Services: International Book Productions Inc.
275 Booth Ave., Toronto ON M4M 2M7

Printed in China

The publisher gratefully acknowledges the financial support for our publishing program by the Government of Canada through the Book Publishing Industry Development Program.

Introduction 8

spring

summer

autumn

winter

introduction

WHILE MY WIFE slept, I dressed in the cold this morning and tiptoed downstairs to put the coffee on. The woodstove was still warm from last night's fire, so it didn't take much to rekindle the flame as I began my morning routine. As I let the dogs out, the radio was playing in the background. It seemed to take a perverse pleasure in describing the snarl of commuter traffic headed into the city, and once again—as I am every morning—I was thankful that we live in the country.

Coffee in hand, I headed outside to the henhouse to collect some eggs and stole a peek inside the sheep barn to count heads. Last week, we spotted a coyote while walking the dogs in the back forty and ever since, we've been wary of predators. Fortunately, everything was as it should be. My rounds completed, I ducked back into the house where the stove was already doing its job. I showered and met my wife at the breakfast table where we reminded each other that we planned to press some apples into cider this weekend. By nine o'clock, I was back upstairs, settling into the editor's chair in my home office as I checked my inbox for messages from *Harrowsmith*'s headquarters.

Harrowsmith Country Life is the magazine for people like me, folks who may not have been born to life in the country but have nevertheless embraced it. I wasn't raised on a farm—I'm a product of the suburbs—but like so many other urban people, I heard the country calling and eagerly left the city to pursue a different way of life. At first, chickens and sheep were the last things on my mind. Indeed, the attraction was the promise of wide open spaces and a relaxed pace of life but, just as our readers so often tell us, the connection to the country soon went deeper than that. Often with no previous experience, country dwellers—my wife and I included—find themselves tilling a vegetable garden, tending a hive of honeybees, tapping maple trees for syrup, building fences and doing all manner of other things for which they are hopelessly ill-prepared. It's reassuring that there is a magazine like *Harrowsmith* to guide them—and us—along.

I've been sitting at the editor's desk since 1997 but *Harrowsmith* goes all the way back to 1976. It was born on James and Elinor Lawrence's kitchen table. They lived near the eastern Ontario village of Camden East and named their new publication after the next town up the highway. As much a labour of love as it was a business venture, *Harrowsmith* tapped into an eager audience of hippie homesteaders, hobby farmers and back-to-the-landers. A decidedly homemade effort, the first issue was short on style but long on chutzpah, providing readers with practical advice on organic farming, wood heat and self-sufficiency. Operating on a shoestring budget, there was some doubt that there would be a second issue, but to everyone's surprise, including the Lawrences', the magazine was a runaway success.

Over the next three decades, the magazine changed with the times and with changes in ownership. Even so, *Harrowsmith* is still the source authority on all matters related to country living, from growing the best organic vegetables to building an energy-efficient home to keeping abreast of rural and environmental issues. Most of all, the magazine remains a great forum for anyone who lives in the country and all those who wish they did. In fact, a significant chunk of the readership is not made up of rural dwellers at all but of people in the city merely watching, fascinated, from the sidelines. A little unsure about how to go about pulling up stakes and making a move to the country, they often write to us at *Harrowsmith*.

Perhaps this book, a compilation of some of our more memorable stories from the past few years, will be the catalyst they need. And for those already living the dream, it can provide further inspiration and affirmation. This book is a celebration of country life and a salute to kindred spirits. And too, for me, it's a reminder that rural living is an acquired skill. Indeed, I remember my skepticism at the prospect of building an outdoor bake oven from roadside clay, but I changed my tune when it produced its very first mouth-watering pizza. And I remember a similar sense of amazement when I helped to build a stone fence using absolutely no mortar. Perhaps this is the most fulfilling thing about life in the country—there are always new things to learn—things that I would never have experienced if I were still living in the city. This is what makes lighting the fire in the morning all the more worthwhile!

Tom Cruickshank

Editor, *Harrowsmith Country Life*

Bewdley, Ontario

spring

spring planning

SPRING IS THE season in which ambitions are realized. After a winter spent indoors, mulling over any number of ideas for gardening and home improvements, the warmer days of spring are a signal that it's time to put those plans into action. But where to start?

For country dwellers, the springtime routine usually begins with seeds. Long before the snow melts, you'll find enthusiasts tending their seedlings under the indoor grow lights, anticipating the day when those fledgling tomatoes, sweet peppers and other veggies can at last be transplanted to the soil. But spring chores don't start in earnest until the arrival of the first glorious sunny day that is warm enough to work outside in shirt sleeves, raking the soil, mixing in compost and otherwise preparing the garden beds. Concurrently, it's time to assess home-maintenance projects, such as painting and roofing, if not entirely new additions or renovations. And for the truly ambitious, springtime is the right time to embark on planning on a larger scale: how best to use your acreage and how best to use its resources.

To some, all this sounds like so much work, but for most of us who live in the country, it's all part of the scheme. Rural dwellers take great pride in their homes and gardens—indeed, for many, the homestead is their major hobby. Its rewards lie in the pleasure of a job well done and the satisfaction of contributing one's own efforts to the project.

Spring, pundits say, is also the best time of year in which to start scanning the real estate pages in search of a country home. Not only is it the season in which homeowners plot their next move, it is also the time of year in which sellers can do little to disguise soggy swampland or wet basements. However, those looking for bargains are apt to be disappointed, for contrary to what you might suspect, hobby farms aren't always a bargain. Prices are on the rise and properties within striking distance of a major city can easily be beyond all but the deepest pockets. Alas, it is not uncommon to spend the same—dollar for dollar—for a 50-acre farm as you would for a downtown condo. However, the news is more encouraging if you're prepared to venture further from the madding crowd. But just how far are you willing to go? Taxes are decidedly lower out in the boonies, but municipal services (police and fire protection, garbage collection, road maintenance) aren't nearly as comprehensive as they are in more populated rural areas, leaving many would-be country dwellers reconsidering the idea.

Moreover, it is a myth to assume that country life is cheaper than it is back in the city. Hydro is more expensive, but the single biggest shock to the pocketbook is transportation, especially for families toting kids to band practice, sleepovers and hockey games in town. At times, a private little country hideaway can seem a long way from civilization. Just imagine how isolated you might feel during a winter snowstorm.

But then, there's the promise of spring. One whiff of the fresh scented air of the awakening earth and all the dilemmas of country life are forgotten.

Every Home Should Have One

by Tom Cruickshank

WITH A DEVOUT commitment to low-impact living, Anthony and Mary Ketchum aren't connected to the power grid. Powering their home is second nature to them, but it has been known to leave others baffled. The couple loves to tell the story of the wayward meter reader who dropped in one day on his rounds. "He could see the lights on in the house, and we could see him scratching his head, looking in vain for the meter," recalls Mary. Exasperated, the visitor finally knocked on the door. "I told him we generate our own power, so there was no meter to read." Bewildered, he muttered, "I see," and turned to leave. With second thoughts and a furrowed brow, he cast his glance back to Mary and asked, "Are you sure?"

Wedged into the side of a hill, Anthony and Mary Ketchum's earth-sheltered home incorporates scores of energy-saving features ideal for off-the-grid living.

Of course, she was sure. Perhaps the hapless meter reader, if he knew about off-the-grid living at all, couldn't fathom that such an attractive and obviously comfortable dwelling would function without conventional electricity. Perhaps he pictured the primitive back-to-the-land stereotype: a makeshift homestead lit by kerosene lamps and serviced by an outhouse. "Lots of people still hold onto that old stereotype," says Anthony, "but we'd like to demonstrate that it's no longer true."

ANTHONY COMES BY his commitment honestly. One of six kids, he and his family enjoyed a cabin in cottage country. "Canoe in, canoe out. No electricity. No plumbing. Now, that was primitive," he recalls. Still, no one felt like they were missing anything. "There was something satisfying about chopping our own wood, catching our own fish and cooking our meals outdoors. When the cabin was struck by lightning in 1967, my brothers and sisters and I were proud to rebuild it using our own skills." As the years went by, he and Mary lived in a conventional Toronto home, embracing their share of creature comforts, but maintaining a reverence for the conservation ethic. Perhaps it was a natural progression that, when it came time to build a house in the country, their zeal for low-impact living became the driving force in their plans.

In 1995, the empty-nest Ketchums acquired a four-acre parcel of wooded land that was part of Mary's parents' estate. Rampant with cedars and sumac, the property was a "leftover" site, rising abruptly some 40 feet (12 m) above the roadside. "My father liked its natural beauty, but by all accounts, it was too steep for building," Mary says. "But what a view!"

Indeed, the land, nestled among the rolling farms and forests of the Oak Ridges Moraine near Orangeville, Ontario, boasts a commanding vista over hills and dales that is quite dramatic, considering that Toronto, a city not known for varied topography, is less than an hour away. "The best view was from relatively level terrain about half way up our hill," offers Anthony. "A local contractor and our friends suggested we ought to build there."

Enter Greg Allen, a design engineer with years of experience in design for sustainable living. "The first thing he did was convince us that the chosen site was wrong," Anthony continues. Sure, the view was nice, but the orientation was unsuitable. "If we were going to power our home with solar energy, a southern exposure was critical. Our original site faced northwest, so we

The hillside location scores points for its role in energy conservation. Bonus: to make the job of adjusting the rooftop photovoltaic cells easier, all Anthony has to do is walk up the rise and step onto the roof.

would have to find another, facing the sun, even though the very steep hillside was a huge constraint."

Greg had an ace up his sleeve that not only turned the awkward location into an advantage, but also satisfied the Ketchums' decree for the responsible use of resources. He proposed to build an earth-shelter house, adopting an innovative type of construction that would actually burrow into the hillside. Only two of the walls (the south and west) are visible, while the others are buried. The fill from the excavation was spread around to provide a level front yard and from the top of the hill, you can step onto the roof.

"But what really sold us on an earth-shelter home," says Anthony, "was the energy savings." Because the north and east walls are below grade, the house is buffered against the wind and, best of all, it benefits from the consistent heat from the soil. "Below the frost line, the earth is a constant 50°F (10°C), year round. We tap into this free heat in winter, and conversely, it helps to keep the house cool in summer."

W ITH ITS FLAT roof (cobblestone over an impenetrable membrane) and attractive pale stucco finish, the house looks bold and stylish, a kind of Santa Fe retro Art Deco adapted to the Ontario countryside. But even the most pleasing components have a function related to low-impact living. For example, the windows aligned along the west and south walls do more than let in the view—they are integral to passive solar. "On a cold winter day, they flood the house with enough sunshine that there's less reliance on our wood fire," says Anthony. Treated with a special thermal coating, they actually have insulating value.

While there is a conventional well for drinking water, the roof is designed with enough of a slope to drain rainwater toward a 2,000 gallon (7,600 l) in-ground cistern for laundry and shower use. Meanwhile, skylights—canted to maximize exposure to the sun—are another solar collector, directing sunlight toward special metal louvres that heat the hot-water tank. Even the rustic pergola, laced with grapevines, is more than decorative—it shelters the exposed walls from summer heat and in winter, without leaves, lets the sunshine in when it is needed most.

Reaching for the sky, the wind generator spins some 68 feet (20 m) above its hilltop location.

Opposite: The planter in the living area is more than just an indulgence for indoor green thumbs: it is also a conduit for purifying household grey water.

A view of the kitchen reveals many a trick in the eco-housebuilder's repertoire: The brick masonry heater and cooktop (extreme right); ceramic floors and brick walls to absorb and radiate heat; the solar-powered Sunfrost fridge. Mary keeps a conventional propane stove on hand for summer use when the masonry heater is not in use.

EARTH-SHELTER ARCHITECTURE IS impressive enough, but it isn't the whole story. "We're equally proud of our masonry heater," Anthony boasts, pointing to the wood-burning "fireplace" dead centre in the living room. Not only does it take the edge off a chilly winter night, it doubles as a cookstove. And best of all, the oversized 27-ton brick structure has a great capacity for radiant heat. "Once the bricks get warm from the fire, they stay warm, dispensing heat throughout the living area—the passive solar from the windows is just a bonus." Additionally, the house rests on a concrete slab and has no basement. (Anthony says, "About one-third of household heat is wasted in the cellar, which most families use only for storage.)

The Ketchum home is full of other innovative ways to conserve energy and resources: Ceramic flooring throughout absorbs and retains heat. The solar refrigerator uses only as much electricity as a conventional 60-watt light bulb, and the ingenious cold cupboard in the kitchen keeps cold by opening directly into the adjacent unheated utility room, allowing for storage of such items as butter and condiments. Grey water from sinks and shower funnels into a central filter to catch food particles and other undesirables and then is channelled into a planter containing indoor tropical plants and grasses which largely absorb the impurities. Any remaining water flows outdoors into a small pond/septic system. The composting toilets use no water and are odour free.

W ITH REGARD TO electricity, the Ketchums knew they were going to have to be precise. Like every other solar-dependent homeowner, Mary and Anthony would require a bank of adjustable PV (photovoltaic) panels—mounted on the rooftop to gather energy from the sun—as well as a set of batteries in which to store the power. "The trick is to calculate how many panels and batteries you'll need," explains Anthony. "You start by taking an inventory of all your appliances and electrical gadgets." Even when they crossed off a toaster, a hair dryer, a clothes dryer and other household energy guzzlers, the couple came up short. "This is Canada, after all, and there are times, particularly from December to February, when the sun just doesn't shine enough to produce sufficient power." That's why the couple decided to augment their solar energy with a wind generator. "We have a turbine mounted on a 68-foot (20-m) tower on top of the hill. It sees us through the dark days of winter." On rare occasions when all else fails, a diesel-powered generator, purchased to supply power for the building's construction, stands at the ready.

The two systems meet in the utility room, where Anthony keeps watch over the gauges that monitor the watts available for household use. Some of the power goes directly to the refrigerator, while the lion's share goes to a bank of eight golf-cart batteries. "Our electrical system has never failed us, but you do have to keep an eye on power consumption." For some, that might be a hassle, but it's second nature to the Ketchums. For Anthony, the rewards are both philosophical and financial. "We feel it's important to do our part for the sake of the environment," he muses. "And while it cost about $145 per square foot to build this house—slightly more than a conventional home this size—it's comforting to know that we will never have to pay another utility bill." Maybe someone should tell the meter reader.

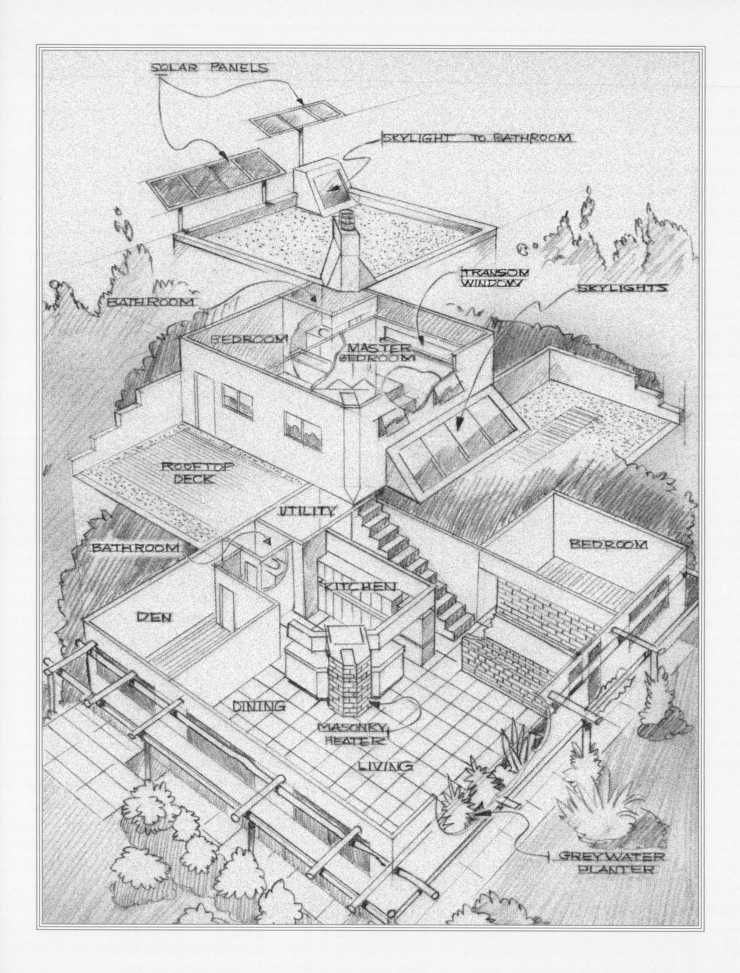

SOLAR PANELS

SKYLIGHT TO BATHROOM

TRANSOM WINDOW

SKYLIGHTS

BATHROOM

BEDROOM

MASTER BEDROOM

ROOFTOP DECK

UTILITY

BATHROOM

BEDROOM

KITCHEN

DEN

DINING

MASONRY HEATER

LIVING

GREYWATER PLANTER

Specs

CONCEPT: Two-storey earth-sheltered home, built into a hillside. Greg Allen and Mario Kani, design engineers. Allen Kani, Toronto.

LOCATION: At the western end of the Oak Ridges Moraine near Orangeville, Ontario.

BEDROOMS: 3

BATHROOMS: 2

TOTAL USABLE FLOOR AREA: 1,600 square feet (149 m²).

FOUNDATION: Concrete slab on grade over poured-concrete footings.

BUILT: 1996, completed 1998.

CONSTRUCTION: Above-grade walls (south and west)—conventional wood frame skeleton, bolstered by steel support posts. Below-grade walls (north and east)—"Durisol" block retaining walls, similar to materials used to construct sound barrier walls along expressways.

CLADDING: Stucco.

ROOF: Cobblestone over impenetrable membrane, with built-in troughs to conduct rainwater run-off to in-ground cistern.

HEATER: Wood-fired masonry heater constructed by Norbert Sent, Shawville, Quebec.

INSULATION: Roxul spun-slag batts (not fibreglass, but recycled from leftover mining slag), to R40.

ELECTRICAL SERVICE: 448-watt solar-powered photovoltaic panels, supplemented by 400-watt wind generator.

WINDOWS: Double-glazed (krypton-gas filled) thermal units, interior panes coated with "heat mirror" finish which insulates to a value of R8.

FLOORS: Ceramic tile throughout (absorbs and retains heat better than wood or other flooring).

WATER SOURCES: Conventional well for drinking water; in-ground cistern for laundry and shower (water gathered from rooftop).

HOT WATER SYSTEM: 90-gallon (340 l) insulated solar-heated tank housed in upstairs closet. System feeds faucets by gravity.

WASTE MANAGEMENT: Two composting toilets. Household grey water dispersed through interior planter with impurities absorbed largely by indoor plants.

Build bird boxes to attract the saw-whet owl, the eastern bluebird and the wood duck (shown clockwise from top left). All three species are cavity-dwellers whose numbers have declined significantly since the mid 1940s. Nesting boxes are one way to help them bounce back.

Boxes for the Birds

by Tim Farquhar

I T'S A JUNGLE out there. Some of our favourite avian friends have it rough at the best of times. Not only do they have to endure the rigours of climate and the threat of predators, they also face tough competition from other species. Humans don't make it any easier: 99 percent of the natural prairie has been ploughed under or paved over, while half of our wetlands have disappeared in the last century. No wonder bird populations are down significantly.

Many dedicated birdwatchers erect boxes on their properties, to offer hard-hit species compensation for the loss of their natural habitat. But not any birdhouse will do. The store-bought variety usually has more appeal for people than birds, because each species is fussy about where it will nest. If the dimensions and location aren't just so, they'll look elsewhere.

With this in mind, here are three bird boxes with very specific measurements, tailor-made to attract the wood duck, the saw-whet owl and the eastern bluebird.

None of the boxes require precision joinery, although the bluebird box, which calls for mitring, demands the most skill. Give it your best shot—the birds will thank you for it.

Tools Required

- Screwdriver
- Mitre box
- Hammer
- Finishing nails
- No. 6 and No. 8 deck screws
- Electric drill
- Table saw

The Wood Duck Box

INDIGENOUS TO every province except Alberta and Newfoundland, the wood duck is often considered Canada's handsomest waterfowl. The drake is easily identified by the distinctive helmet it wears on its head.

Wood ducks like to nest well off the ground, in hollow, lakeside tree trunks or abandoned woodpecker holes. Coaxing their days-old chicks from the nest is no easy task for the female, as it's a long drop to the ground below. But the problem facing the wood duck has less to do with the leap from the nest as it does with the extent to which old logs have disappeared from riverbanks and lakeshores. To keep their populations at historic levels, the wood duck needs help, that is, a box that imitates its natural nesting site

A wood duck nesting box should be mounted about 5–10 feet (1.5–3 m) off the ground and, most importantly, ought to be tilted toward the ground so that the emerging ducklings have an easier time dropping from the nest. A riverside location is ideal, especially a sheltered spot on a mid-stream island, safe from raccoons.

Wood ducks aren't fussy about feathering their own nests, but they do like to snuggle into a soft surface to raise their young. It's a good idea to line the box with wood shavings.

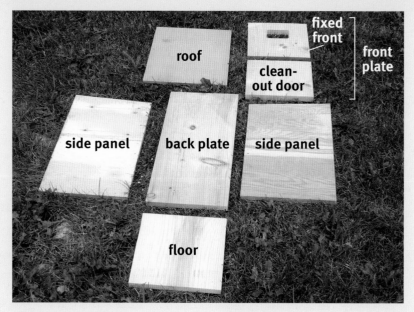

Components

(Unless otherwise noted, all parts are sawn from rough-cut 1″ barnboard or pine. Scraps and off-cuts can be used.)

Roof—⅝″ or ¾″ plywood, 13″ x 17″

Front plate—11″ x 24″, cut in half (see Step 3). Top half is fixed; bottom half functions as clean-out hatch.

Back plate—11″ x 28″

Side panel—⅝″ or ¾″ plywood, 14″ wide, long edge 26″, short edge 24″

Floor—11″ x 12″

Assembly

STEP 1 Fasten side panels to back (a) with 2″ No. 8 deck screws. Fasten floor to sides and back plate. All pieces are attached flush to the outside edge, except the back plate, which extends for installation to a post in the ground.

STEP 2 Cut entry hole in front plate. It measures 3″ x 4″, with long dimension on the horizontal. Bevel the cut so there are no sharp edges (b).

a

c

b

d

STEP 3 Cut the front plate in half, bevelled at a 22° angle. Make sure the cut is aligned so that water drains away from the box (c). Fix the top half of the front plate to box.

STEP 4 With a saw, cut shallow grooves on the inside of the door—the bottom half of the front plate and up to the entry hole—so that ducklings have a foothold upon leaving the nest.

STEP 5 Put one screw through each side of the box, into the door, just below the bevelled top cut. To make the door operable, drill two holes, 2½" deep, ⅛" diameter, at bottom edge. Insert two galvanized nails to act as door locks.

STEP 6 Drill 4 drainage holes, ¾" diameter, in floor. Drill 5 vent holes, ½" diameter, in sides (d).

STEP 7 Attach roof with 2" No. 8 deck screws. Make sure it's flush with the back plate and leave plenty of overhang at the front (e).

e

The Saw-Whet Owl Box

To whet a saw is to put it in a vise for sharpening with a file. Saw-whetting makes a distinct whistle, much like the call of this pixie-sized owl with the big curious eyes. The call is easy for humans to imitate, and you can sometimes get a response if you whistle the right tune in the forest.

Smaller than a robin, the saw-whet is found across southern Canada and is a good owl to have around, since it feeds on pesky insects and small rodents. However, its numbers aren't as strong as they should be because their favourite nesting sites—tree cavities in evergreen woods—are being lost. Nesting boxes encourage the saw-whet, but be warned that this owl is something of a nomad and not guaranteed to return year after year.

The best location for an owl box is 10–20 feet (3–6 m) up in a pine or spruce tree, preferably in a dense thicket of conifers. Line the box with wood shavings or chips. If your box attracts a pair of saw-whets, you'll hear them before you see them.

Components

(All parts sawn from rough-cut 1″ barnboard or pine. Scraps and off-cuts can be used.)

Roof—10″ x 10″ square. Make a ⅛″ deep cut, ¼″ back from one end to form a drip edge.

Floor—6″ x 6 ½″ plus or minus, depending on thickness of wood. Nip off each corner just enough to allow drainage.

Back plate—6″ x 18″

Doorstop—½″ thick x 1 ½″ wide x 10″

Side panel—8″ wide, with one edge cut to 12″ long, the other to 14″. Drill 3 vent holes, ⅝″ diameter, near upper edge.

Door—6″ x 14″. Drill a 2 ½″ diameter hole, about 11″ from the base.

Below the hole, score the inside surface with saw cuts to make toe grips.

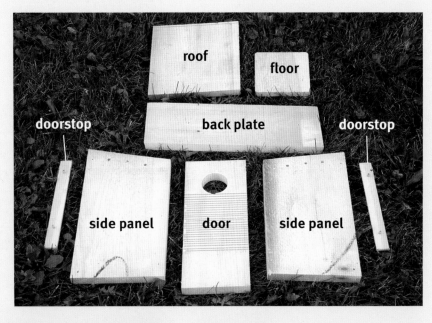

roof

floor

doorstop

back plate

doorstop

side panel

door

side panel

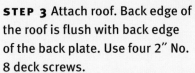

Assembly

STEP 1 Mount a doorstop to the longest dimension of each side panel (a). Allow 1″ for placement of door. Position toward top edge of sides. Use ¾″ No. 6 wood screws.

STEP 2 Mount both sides (b) to outside edges of back plate, using 2″ No. 8 deck screws. Attach the floor 1½″ up from bottom edge of side panels.

STEP 3 Attach roof. Back edge of the roof is flush with back edge of the back plate. Use four 2″ No. 8 deck screws.

STEP 4 Position door with upper edge flush against roof. Drill two screws (c) into sides at the bottom of the door, below floor, to act as hinge.

STEP 5 The door is held in place with one galvanized finishing nail, placed in a drilled hole, which can be removed to open the door for clean-out (d).

The Eastern Bluebird Box

OUR NATIVE eastern bluebird is one of the species that has suffered most from the invasion of the fiercely competitive European starling. However, its decline can also be blamed on loss of nesting sites. It prefers to set up housekeeping in decaying trees and fence posts in meadows and fields, which seem to be in short supply these days. Fortunately, birders have rallied to the cause, building nesting boxes that simulate a natural nesting site. The following box is a variation on the original "Peterson" design, conceived by the same people who publish the Peterson field guides.

Crucial to the success of a bluebird box is the access hole size. Anything larger than 1⅜″ and the box invites starlings (which need no help at all in sustaining their numbers), swallows and other competitors.

The comeback of the eastern bluebird has been slow and not every box is a guaranteed success, but a glimpse of those iridescent colours—sky-blue back and rusty-orange breast—is a sight not soon forgotten.

Bluebirds like to nest in the open. Trees can be nearby, but the crucial factor is to locate the box 5–7 feet (1.5–2 m) off the ground. Birders usually hang more than one box, creating a "bluebird trail" on their properties.

Components

(All parts are 2 x 4 lumber, unless otherwise specified.)

Roof—1 x 10, 13″ long

Top frame member—9″ long, bevelled at 27° on one end and 45° on the other

Bottom frame member—3″ long, bevelled at 27° on one end

Back plate—at least 24″ long, top edge bevelled to 27°

2 Side panels—rough 1″ thick pine, 15″ long on front side, 3″ wide at bottom, 10½″ wide at top. Drill two ¾″ vent holes in line with the entrance hole.

Door—9″ x 13″, top edge mitred to 45°. To configure entrance hole, see Step 1.

Assembly

STEP 1 Drill a 1¾″ hole in the door. Drill a second hole directly beneath the first and chisel out the remaining wood to form a 1¼″ oval entrance hole, vertically aligned. Below the hole, gouge or chisel several grooves on the inside surface to provide toe grips for emerging fledglings.

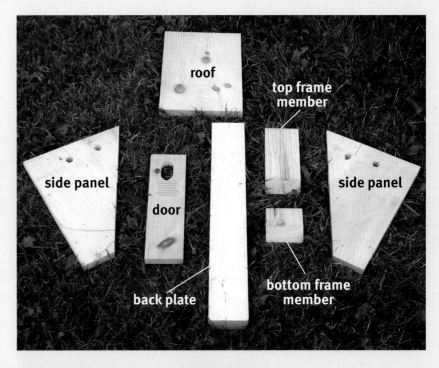

roof

top frame member

side panel

door

side panel

back plate

bottom frame member

STEP 2 Fasten the top frame member to the back plate with two 3" No. 8 deck screws. Join the two 27° ends to each other (a). Fasten the sides to the back plate and top member with four 2" No. 8 deck screws per side.

STEP 3 Insert the bottom frame member (b), aligning the angled edge with the side panels. Position it at a point that allows sufficient room to accommodate the door.

STEP 4 Drop the door into position (c), leaving a ½" to ⅝" gap on the top (mitred) edge for ventilation.

STEP 5 The door is held in place (d) with three galvanized finishing nails—two are driven home near the base to act as pivot points while the third is merely placed in a drilled hole and can be removed to open the door for clean-out.

STEP 6 Attach roof on top frame (e) with 2" No. 8 deck screws.

The Un-Garden

by Craille Maguire Gillies

THEY WERE MARGINAL lands at best, and, by the 1940s, the flat plains of eastern Ontario were looking the worse for wear. A century of agricultural exploitation had turned vast stretches into virtual deserts. Intensively farmed, with hardly a thought to the future, there was little natural vegetation to stabilize the soil. Sand dunes grew as high as second-storey barns. The natural drainage was blocked by roads, creating quagmires and swamps. The landscape supported only the hardiest plants and almost no wildlife.

Fast-forward four decades. In the early 1980s, Philip Fry, an art historian and professor of fine arts at the University of Ottawa—passionate about native plants and concerned about regional habitat destruction—began to revitalize one such parcel of damaged land. Founded on the horticultural ideology sometimes referred to as "un-gardening," Philip Fry's 15 acres put the environment first.

Under a canopy of shade, Philip Fry tends seedlings in his native-plant nursery.

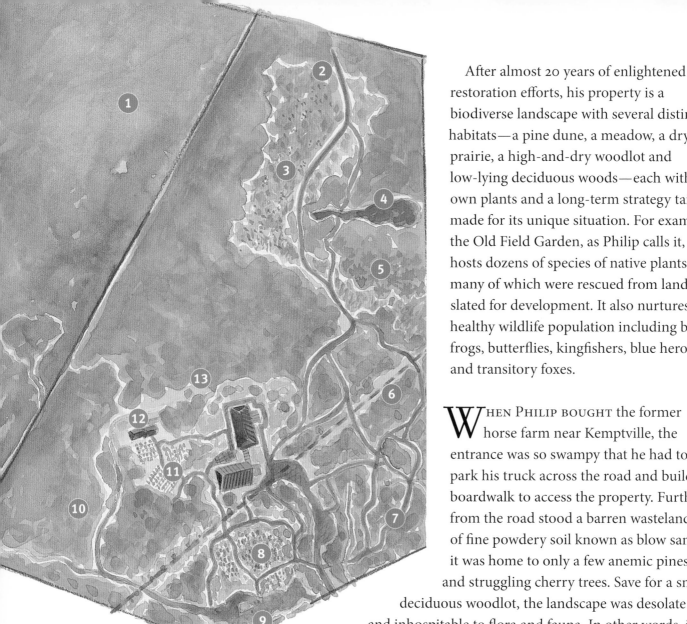

To date, about half of Philip's 15 acres have been treated to his restorative touch. Meanwhile, the cedar woodlot is regenerating on its own.

1 cedar woodlot
2 upper deciduous wood
3 prairie
4 upper pond
5 pine dune
6 hydro right of way
7 lower deciduous wood
8 meadow
9 lower pond
10 dogwood swamp
11 nursery
12 potting sheds
13 fern gully

After almost 20 years of enlightened restoration efforts, his property is a biodiverse landscape with several distinct habitats—a pine dune, a meadow, a dry prairie, a high-and-dry woodlot and low-lying deciduous woods—each with its own plants and a long-term strategy tailor-made for its unique situation. For example, the Old Field Garden, as Philip calls it, hosts dozens of species of native plants, many of which were rescued from lands slated for development. It also nurtures a healthy wildlife population including bull-frogs, butterflies, kingfishers, blue herons and transitory foxes.

WHEN PHILIP BOUGHT the former horse farm near Kemptville, the entrance was so swampy that he had to park his truck across the road and build a boardwalk to access the property. Further from the road stood a barren wasteland of fine powdery soil known as blow sand; it was home to only a few anemic pines and struggling cherry trees. Save for a small deciduous woodlot, the landscape was desolate and inhospitable to flora and fauna. In other words, it was perfect. "The place was bad enough to be quite exciting," quips Philip, recalling the challenge that lay ahead. His goal was to make the land look natural again, as if settlers had never intervened. If the land had been left to its own devices, however, it would have taken several lifetimes to get results, so here and there, Philip lent Mother Nature a hand. In environmental circles, this is known as habitat gardening or un-gardening, the very antithesis of the conventional manicured garden. (The concept was first coined by Sarah Stein, an environmental advocate and author of *Noah's Garden*.) But don't be fooled, the unplanned, uncultivated look requires just as much perseverance and dedica-tion as a perennial border or a bed of roses.

Philip spent the first year walking the grounds, observing conditions such as light and soil, and documenting problems such as drainage. "Assessment is the first step," Philip advises, "because once you know what you've got, then you know what you can do." One of his initial tasks was to assess the existing drainage pattern. For help with this, he recruited faculty from the university's geography department. They used biodegradable red dye in the water to map its flow through the property and noted that farm lanes had obstructed natural drainage.

Eventually, the problem was resolved by the creation of a pond. "It became a host not only to plant life, but aquatic life as well," says Philip.

Elsewhere, he thinned dense patches of scrub and eastern white cedar and reintroduced poplar, ash, elm and other pioneer trees, since these are the first to colonize abandoned farmland naturally as it gradually reverts to forest. In the deciduous woods, drainage channels were dug and thousands of woodland flowers and groundcovers were planted. In a grove of pines, wood chips were spread over the ground to stabilize the humus-starved soil, while white, red and jack pine saplings were introduced to diversify the woodland and prevent further erosion.

D ESPITE INITIAL SUCCESS with the pond and pine grove, overall progress was slow and the work continues to this day. Philip and a devoted group of volunteers have also rescued a rare and sensitive variety of lady's slipper called moccasin flower (*Cypripedium acaule*) from a site that stood in the way of development. "It's taken 15 years for our grounds to regenerate themselves to the point where something as fussy as the moccasin flower can flourish," he says. "But that's one of the rewards of un-gardening."

Similar rescue missions have supplied the garden with lots of plant material, with Philip and his volunteers often working against time to save endangered local flora. Their success rate is astonishing: In 1992, more than 10,000 ferns, saplings and woodland flowers were moved out of harm's way when lands were torn up for the construction of nearby Highway 416, a new freeway linking Highway 401 to Ottawa. Supported by the provincial Ministry of Natural Resources, Philip's group spent an entire summer relocating plants such as the maidenhair fern (*Adiantum pedatum*), foamflower (*Tiarella cordifolia*) and sharp-lobed hepatica (*Hepatica acutiloba*). These were transferred to the newly established deciduous woods at the Old Field Garden. Eventually, the transplants naturalized under an umbrella of pine and birch.

The rare pink lady's slipper now flourishes in the un-garden.

Philip uses his native flowers to measure the garden's ecological health. "Many native plants are highly sensitive to changes in habitat, which means that they do not do well if you take them away from the animals, insects and other plants to which they are accustomed in nature." A good example is the connection between hummingbirds and cardinal flowers (*Lobelia cardinalis*). "Hummingbirds adore red, and the cardinal flower is one of the few absolutely red plants on earth. It has the nectar the hummingbird needs, and the bird pollinates the plant. One can't flourish without the other—it's a very simple ecological relationship, but an important one."

To give his rehabilitation project a head start, Philip originally created a nursery to germinate and propagate wildflowers, but relied on it less and less as the grounds became well enough established to let nature take its course. "Wherever possible, I like letting things occur naturally—it encourages biodiversity," he says, reminding himself of his raison d'être, "and biodiversity is what it's all about." Well aware of the relationships between the loss of habitat, species extinction and the decline in biodiversity, Philip sees his Old Field Garden as a way of fighting back. "The world loses species every day because we continue to clear natural lands and let our cities grow unabated—it's a daunting problem until you realize that you can make a difference." Thinking of how his rehabilitated land rose from the dead, he adds, "The answer begins in your own backyard."

A makeshift fortress of twigs ensures that a jack-in-the-pulpit has a fighting chance.

Philip Fry's Habitat Strategies

Ponds

OVER THE DECADES, the concession road had been graded higher and higher, eventually damming the natural drainage pattern and blocking entry to the property. Philip's solution: In 1985, the bog was excavated into a 70- x 130-foot (21- x 39-m) pond, whose borders followed the natural contours of the land. A second pond, dug by hand in an already wet area in the northern reaches of the property, came later. "It was a poorly drained spot that was a haven for mosquitoes," explains Philip. The excavation, contained naturally by the underlying hardpan soil, is deep enough to support a healthy minnow population, which keeps mosquito larvae at bay. Both ponds soon became garden central for wildlife.

Blue Flag iris and Fragrant waterlily flourish in Philip's lower pond habitat.

When creating a pond, Philip advises homeowners to avoid what is called "bathtub" edges. "They are as useless to a habitat as they are awkward and ugly." Instead, he recommends multi-levelled ledges to suit different aquatic, shallow and shoreline species, along with providing some shady areas to protect tadpoles from sun.

Meadow

THE GRASS IS always greener over the septic tank, and the soil a little wetter, too—which provided a logical starting point for Philip to build a meadow. About to be overrun by the relentless invasion of cedars, the site, which slopes toward one of the ponds, was also a natural for a floral display because it was in plain view of the living room window.

Prominent in the mélange of wildflowers and grasses are tough natives such as coneflowers and sylphiums, which were introduced gradually and nurtured with plenty of well-rotted horse manure. Just as white cedar is the bane of the woodlots, the enemy here is wild grape, whose broad leaves and reckless habits can quickly smother more desirable plants.

Pine Dune

"THE SOIL HERE was so thin that I could scoop it up with my hand," Philip says of the dune on which only a few scruffy pines and cherry saplings grew. To enhance the environs and nurture a healthy groundcover and understorey (the layer of vegetation beneath the main canopy of a forest), Philip unleashed a secret weapon: mulch. He carpeted the area in wood chips, which proved just the helping hand needed to simulate the branch litter and decaying limbs in which woodland flowers thrive. Next, he enhanced existing plantings with white, red and jack pines. Falling needles from the conifers create an acidic soil, much appreciated by three kinds of Solomon's seal (*Polygonatum biflorum*), interrupted fern (*Osmunda clatoniana*), wild ginger (*Asarum caudatum*) and other exotic-sounding native plants now found on the dune.

Prairie

MEADOWS AND PRAIRIES are not the same animal. "There's a fundamental difference," explains Philip. By its very nature, a prairie is a dry environment, while a meadow has more water available to it. "The difference shows in the species indigenous

Mulch was a key ingredient in enhancing the pine barrens.

Opposite: Philip's refurbished meadow overflows with such native wildflowers as purple coneflower and black-eyed Susans.

to each." Bottle gentians, for example, need the moisture that only a meadow can provide, and don't stand a chance against the prairie brown-eyed Susans.

Toward the north end of the property lay a high, dry clearing on a foot and a half (0.5 m) of sand, perfect to develop into a prairie. Adopting a less-is-more approach, Philip resisted the urge to introduce personal favourites that would not occur naturally. "Meadows and prairies should be created judiciously," he says. "The best idea is to work with what is already growing on the site, not clearing it out with herbicides and broadcasting seed willy-nilly."

Upper Deciduous Woods

Now HOME TO more than 12,000 salvaged woodland plants, the success of the upper deciduous woods—a higher, drier corner of the property—surprised ecologists at the Ontario Ministry of Natural Resources. Once overrun by cedars, the area is now diverse enough to support red and white trilliums, blue cohosh (*Caulophyllum thalictroides*) and trout lily (*Erythronium americanus*). But when disaster struck, Philip was worried that his success would be short-lived. "The infamous ice storm of January 1998 reduced hundreds of new trees to mere twigs," he reveals. Much to his surprise, the habitat bounced back quickly. With some judicious pruning, crowns that were laden with ice rebounded nicely, while trees that had snapped in half have since started to grow new leader branches.

Lower Deciduous Woods

BY THE TIME Philip arrived in the 1980s, eastern white cedar had overtaken most of the abandoned farm property. "It is a highly competitive species," Philip remarks, adding that he once counted 100 seedlings on a single square-foot patch. "They grow so densely that everything else is squeezed out."

Over time, the cedar would eventually succumb to other woodland species, but to allow the competition a head start, Philip selectively thinned out the bush to create "light chimneys" that would give deciduous saplings a fighting chance. A heaping helping of horse manure delivered the knockout punch, allowing a mixture of maples, basswood, hickory and birch to gain a foothold. "The red maples, which don't mind getting their feet wet in the low areas, are 15 feet high now," he reports, "and grow up to 18 inches a year."

Red maples and other hardwoods in the lower deciduous woods provide a dappled canopy in which maidenhair ferns can thrive.

Opposite: A shady path winds through the upper deciduous woods, now home to many transplanted woodland plants.

Country Dreaming

A *Harrowsmith Country Life* Staff Report

S OME PEOPLE ARE born city rats. They thrive on the kind of hustle and bustle that you can only find in the metropolis and are destined to live their entire lives in the concrete jungle. There is, however, another breed—the country mouse. One who feels more at home surrounded by nature than other people. One who would prefer to stay home rather than fight for a parking spot downtown. One who longs to pick fresh lettuce from her garden rather than buying that limp stuff in plastic bags. One who wants to split his own firewood rather than pay a gas bill every month.

Being happy with a move from the city to the country means finding just the right homestead to suit your personality and your needs.

Unfortunately, many of these erstwhile country mice actually live in cities. They dream of the day when they'll finally be able to chuck the city job, bid their too-close neighbours adieu, and buy a little house in the country somewhere. But day after day, year after year, they continue to suppress their claustrophobia, brave the crowds and mutter obscenities as they fight rush-hour traffic.

Why do they stay? Perhaps it's because they feel their dream life is too idyllic to be possible. Or perhaps they feel so overwhelmed by uncertainty—Could we really make it work? Should we take that chance? What if it's a bad choice?—that they can't bring themselves to make the decision to move to the country. Then again, perhaps they don't realize that living in the city is a choice, too.

To BE FAIR, many feel certain that they can't afford to move to the country. Certainly, people who own a house in the city are sitting on an investment that continues to increase in value. Why would they sell? Well, for one thing, that house anchors them to a lifestyle that may not be as satisfying as they would like. If they bite the bullet, they could afford a gorgeous country property for a fraction of the sale price. Indeed, country real estate can cost far less than an ordinary house on a small suburban lot. The net profit could make a tidy nest egg for their retirement, allow them to improve the new property, or provide for a welcome increase in their monthly budget.

Another realistic hitch in the plan to leave the city is the problem of finding a good job "out there." Indeed, in some lines of work, such as hi-tech research and specialized medicine, career paths may be limited to the urban core. In other fields, such as teaching, law, nursing, medicine and policing, rural recruits are sorely needed. Various professionals may also find it easier to find an opening in their chosen rural locale, where there are fewer qualified candidates than in the big city. What's more, large manufacturing corporations have started to decentralize, setting up smaller facilities in rural locations where the rent is cheaper; additionally, there are many niche markets that remain unexploited for self-employed entrepreneurs. Working from home is another option—if your job already has you working alone on a computer for most of the workday, there's no reason why you can't telecommute from your home office instead, using the telephone, fax and email to stay in the loop.

There are as many ways to make the leap from city to country living as there are back roads from one village to another. The timid may prefer to wade in without severing their ties too soon—they could lease their city place and commute to work from a rented country house. As they grow more comfortable with their choice of rural locale, they can try compressing their workweek into three days instead of five, or working from home a couple of days a week. They can use their rural rental home as a base from which to explore the area, investigate job prospects and look for a suitable home to buy.

FINDING YOUR PLACE in the country can be a slow process. Where do you start? One tack is to make a list of criteria: Write down everything you can think of to describe your dream property, and then divide it into "must haves" and "would be nice to haves." Be sure to define the property size and price range. Other factors, such as the house's proximity to the road and other houses, the scenic quality of the view, the age of the house and the state of repair of the outbuildings are factors that may also come into play.

How far from the madding crowd do you want to go? Some people move to the country in search of that small-town community feeling, and are happy in a town of 5,000 to 10,000 residents or even a tight-knit village of 200. Others want a place of their own in the countryside. If you would like a larger property but are a bit of a nervous Nellie, look for a place near the road, so you can see the neighbours' reassuring lights after dark. If, however, you wish to sunbathe in the nude or sing off-key at the top of your lungs while you walk the dogs, without making anybody laugh, look for a place out in the middle of nowhere, with lots of land, surrounded by equally large holdings on all sides. Extreme privacy is also available, at a cost—extending the road, power and phone lines to a house out in the bush may not be an option for anyone but a zillionaire.

Keep in mind that too much land can become a real headache. Fields must be mown so they don't get weedy, drainage ditches must be kept functioning properly, and kilometres of fencing must be maintained. Ponds must be drained and re-dug every so often to keep them from getting shallow and mucky, streams cleared of washed-up debris that dams them, long driveways graded and ploughed, dying trees felled and chopped into firewood, gigantic lawns mowed, and so on. If you buy a larger acreage than you really need, its stewardship can easily keep you too busy to enjoy living there.

ONCE YOU'VE DEFINED what you want, narrow down the search perimeter. Choose a particular region first of all, and then select a few lovely municipalities within that area before approaching a local real estate agent. And then, even when you think you've found a great house, think again before you sign on the dotted line. A wreck of a house can be completely renovated and an overgrown property landscaped, but the surrounding area is out of your control. Therefore, choose your location even more wisely than you choose your house.

Prowl nearby roads to get a feel for the district, looking for potential nuisances like garbage bags dumped in the ditches, evidence of large-scale logging in the forest surrounding your

To maintain a healthy pond, one that supports a variety of aquatic plants such as beautiful water lilies, it must be drained and re-dug every now and then.

Tips for the Rural Greenhorn

DO not put up an impenetrable fence along the front of your property, especially if you live on a quiet country road. This will only make you look like a snob, if not a drug dealer. If you need privacy, plant trees.

DO plant a small vegetable garden. There's nothing like the flavour of homegrown garlic, basil and red leaf lettuce. Tomatoes and zucchini are other essential crops for the home garden. While you're at it, why not throw in a few potatoes, some butternut squash, and a couple of rows of beans?

DON'T make your garden too large to tend. Start with a 10' x 10' (3 m x 3 m) area and learn to take care of it; then, expand gradually each year as you get the hang of it.

DO mulch your garden. It's the easiest way to keep it weed free. Spread a few inches of straw (not hay), wood chips, or other weed-free organic matter in midsummer, once the seeds you planted have sprouted. Otherwise, the gazillions of weed seeds already in the soil will sprout and take over your garden faster than you can call for help.

DO put up a hammock. Every so often, take the time to lie back and watch the clouds change shape or the stars rotate through the sky.

DO ask for advice, but don't become a burden. You will certainly need help with all the jobs that come with a country property, but understand that your neighbours have chores of their own and expect others to be self-sufficient.

DON'T put too much stock in the idea of digging a pond. Just about every country dweller dreams of a cool, crystal-clear swimming hole tucked behind the house, but few properties are blessed with a source of running water abundant enough to keep it clean and fresh in the dead of summer. A backhoe operator will be happy to oblige any flight of fancy as long as you're footing the bill, but you're the one who'll be left with a mucky, leech-infested mud pit.

DON'T neglect your chimney. It must be kept in tip-top shape and cleaned once a year.

DON'T burn softwoods or "green" hardwood. The logs must have dried sufficiently to crack at the ends. Dry firewood burns with a crackling sound, not a squeaky sizzle.

DO compost your kitchen scraps and non-woody garden trimmings. Compost is the best fertilizer for your tomatoes and roses, it's free, and it helps you reduce the number of bags of garbage you produce every week.

DO be on the lookout for rabies. If you spot an animal that is acting strangely, such as a fox that appears to have no fear of you or a dog that's staggering around foaming at the mouth, it may be rabid.

DO keep a stock of bottled water, matches, candles, lamp oil and flashlight batteries for when the power goes out.

DO discourage thieves who prey on "fancy" country houses owned by city people. Put in an alarm system, install a timer for the lights, and park a car in the driveway. If you're going to be away, hire someone trustworthy to make the place look occupied—this person should do things like pick up the mail, drive into the driveway every day to make tire tracks and pick up any fallen tree limbs or lawn furniture that has blown over.

DON'T expect municipal services such as recycling, high-speed Internet, cable, or public transit. Depending on where you settle, you may luck out with one or two of these, but find out before you relocate.

DON'T let your dog wander. Yes, wide-open spaces seem like nirvana for leashed city dogs, but a loose dog can make a real nuisance of itself. If it doesn't get hit by a car, it may get into the neighbour's garbage, harass livestock, or team up with other dogs and chase deer. If that's the case, it will be summarily shot.

DO be generous with your bounty—offer your neighbours divisions of your perennials, bottles of your home-grown raspberry jam, and use of your swimming hole or woodland trails. They will return the favour in their own way.

Alpacas are becoming popular on hobby farms such as on Treasurebrook Farm near Durham, Ontario. These curious creatures are kept both for their beautiful wool and as breeding stock.

THERE'S NO QUESTION that when you leave the city, you also leave behind a certain level of cultural diversity. Not only will your neighbours become more homogeneous in terms of race, language, religion and political beliefs, but so will your shopping and restaurant options. You may be loath to say goodbye to a city offering fresh Chilean empanadas and imported Italian suits, but ask yourself: How often do you actually seek out funky shops and ethnic eateries? More often than not, we wind up frequenting chain stores and restaurants instead—whatever's nearby and has ample parking.

Ethnic restaurants may be few and far between in the countryside, but they do exist—sometimes in the strangest of places. Likewise, you may have to ferret out the good bookstores, libraries and art galleries. Once you've found them, you may not miss the city at all.

In a similar vein, you may think that if you move to the country, you'll have to forsake cultural outings such as the symphony, opera and ballet, not to mention NHL games. It is true that you'll no longer live in the same milieu as these institutions, but does that necessarily mean you'll frequent them any less often? Anything worth a hundred-dollar ticket is worth driving into the city to see, *n'est-ce pas*?

Besides, there is a great deal of culture in the countryside, too. Sure, some of it may be culture with a small *c*, such as summer theatre and crafts, but scratch the surface, and you'll find more artists per capita than in any given downtown city core. Painters, sculptors, writers and composers flee to the countryside for exactly the same reasons as you: natural beauty to inspire their work, peace and quiet in which to concentrate, and the space to build a customized, private workshop. A local studio tour or art festival is a great way to acquaint yourself with their work, and maybe even meet them in person. By the same token, there's no reason to give up on the groups and clubs you enjoyed in the city—there are plenty of country residents who like to play cards, read novels and study a second language.

If you are a sports' enthusiast, and you're willing to drive a little, you will find golf courses galore, as well as mountain biking or skiing trails, softball, hockey and soccer leagues, tennis and squash courts, curling and bowling tournaments, master's swimming teams, and almost anything else that the fit-conscious body could desire.

Living in the country opens other new doors, too. Out there, you have the space to embark on projects you've always dreamed of, whether that's building a dance studio in the barn, erecting a dressage ring next to the stables, or stocking a pond with sport fish to practise angling. A pet lover can indulge a penchant for large breeds and give the beast all the space it needs to really stretch its legs. A hobby farmer at heart can raise alpacas, donkeys, geese, or even sheep and other livestock. An amateur naturalist can't help but get to know the environs through all their incremental seasonal changes. And every once in a while, even a workaholic can try taking it easy for a spell—afternoon naps on the screened-in porch are absolutely de rigueur. Moving to the country is not just a relocation, it is a lifestyle change.

Homestead Sweet Homestead

by Bridget Wayland

OW MUCH LAND do you really need? It's a question everyone entertains at one time or another when dreaming about life in the country. Luckily, the short answer seems to be: Not as much as you might think. Even the most unassuming property can provide enough veggies and fruit for a family year-round. Likewise, a pond need not be the size of a lake to supply a year's worth of fresh fish. And augmenting your income with a part-time farming venture is possible with even a modest parcel of arable land.

What follows are a few ideas for making good use of your land, whether you have a small acreage or more property than you know what to do with. These three hypothetical plans for country properties are intended to demonstrate a realistic scenario for 5, 10 or 40 acres, all practicalities considered.

Even a modest five-acre homestead can still be large enough to provide you and your family with vegetables and fruits year-round.

God's Little Acre: Under Five Acres

Subsistence, or niche, market farming

A SMALL PIECE OF land is a gold mine of possibilities. If you're agriculturally minded, five acres of fertile soil is more than enough to support a small-scale commercial endeavour. In fact, in British Columbia, five-acre lots are fast becoming the most popular size for the new type of agricultural entrepreneur — someone wishing to capitalize on a high-profit niche market, such as organic vegetable or fruit production, gourmet mushrooms, cut flowers or potted plants. In intensive, efficient cultivation, these horticultural avenues can provide significant additional income, but may demand more time than some part-time farmers are willing to put in.

Commercial possibilities aside, a five-acre homestead can be your own small piece of paradise, requiring as much or as little work as you're prepared to put into it. There's ample space around the house for a sunny expanse of green lawn, extensive perennial beds and a row of majestic shade trees. Make your vegetable garden and berry patch as large as you like — it can provide ample produce for the dinner table, plus plenty of extras for jellies, pickles and preserves. All this can be done without purchasing significant machinery, except perhaps for renting a heavy-duty Rototiller for the vegetable garden.

A small acreage does not lend itself to livestock, although there's enough room on five acres for a few geese and a flock of free-range hens. And your family will get all the apples, pears, cherries and plums they can eat from a small orchard established behind the house. At the rear of the property, a mixed stand of mature trees will provide you with privacy, shade and a wildlife habitat, and make a natural playground for kids and visiting grandchildren.

Three fruit trees of any one type: apple, pear, plum, cherry, and any nut tree that will grow in your climate zone will provide a harvest bounteous enough for the whole neighbourhood. For your own sanity, choose varieties that mature at staggered intervals.

Ducks and geese will be delighted with a small water pond and portable duck house.

Guest cottage is a godsend in summer when city friends and far-flung relatives descend upon your idyllic retreat. It can also make a dandy home office.

Try blueberries, raspberries and strawberries in the berry patch. There is nothing on this earth better than a warm, sun-sweetened strawberry.

A potting shed makes it easier to manage a large vegetable garden and berry patch. Could double as a workshop or studio.

Sugar maples provide shade and an opportunity to tap them in spring. You don't need a forest of maples to enjoy the pleasures of making your own maple syrup.

A line of conifers provides a windbreak on the windward side of the property.

Position beehives near the orchard to pollinate the fruit trees in spring. They'll forage in neighbours' fields the rest of the summer.

A peaceful walking trail winds through the orchard and into the woods. Woodlot is too small to provide a sustainable supply of firewood to heat your home.

Chickens need just enough shelter close to the house to keep them safe from predators and out of the weather. Give them an enclosed run to scratch for bugs, weed seedlings and gravel.

Try a few cherry tomato plants in the herb garden, conveniently placed just outside the kitchen.

The compost heap is located close to the house for easy access.

The house and patio are surrounded by perennial flower beds and ornamental plantings.

The vegetable garden is big enough for corn, potatoes, pumpkins and anything else you choose to plant.

Down on the Farm:
10 to 15 Acres

"Pick-Your-Own" fruit and vegetable production; one or two horses

YOU MIGHT NOT think a 15-acre lot is a big plot of land, but think again. There's enough land to produce organic garlic, leeks or asparagus for distribution through a CSA (community shared agriculture). Even with as few as 10 acres, a commercial pick-your-own corn or strawberry operation is feasible. So is a large farm pond, to be used for irrigation and cooling down after weeding the garden. You'll also have the option to house larger livestock, such as a horse or two or a milk cow, whose copious manure is a godsend for the gardens. Mind you, the property cannot support larger herds.

Of course, grazing animals require pasture. It'll take several acres to grow enough alfalfa hay to get two horses through the winter. Don't forget about crop rotation and green manuring, a simple way to maintain soil fertility without adding commercial fertilizer. Or if you're not willing to invest in the machinery and headache of haying and crop rotation, it's easy enough to purchase hay and straw. In that case, you can use the acreage to make the orchard bigger, for extra woodland, or to establish a wildflower meadow.

While this property is not large enough for a productive woodlot, a few forested acres will provide a bit of private wilderness to explore on foot, cross-country skis and horseback. Songbirds and woodpeckers will nest in the woods, and small animals like voles, porcupines and rabbits will find shelter along its edges. These will in turn attract owls, hawks and other birds of prey, for rather exciting birdwatching. While you'll have a heck of a time keeping deer out of the garden, your dog will feel useful keeping them at bay.

And, of course, if you're not agriculturally inclined, you can always plant native trees and transform your acreage into a wooded wonderland, surrounding yourself with the sights and sounds of nature, for maximum privacy and creative inspiration.

Conifer windbreak shelters vegetables and berries.

The vegetable garden can be as large as you can handle.

Firewood is stacked behind the garage in a woodshed that keeps the rain off but allows air to circulate on three sides.

Compost bin tucked up against garage.

Pick-your-own berries and sweet corn.

Shade trees cool the south side of the house in summer.

Roadside stand for excess berries and corn can attract drive-by customers.

Ornamental flower beds and shrubs pretty up the yard. Keep an herb garden by the kitchen door.

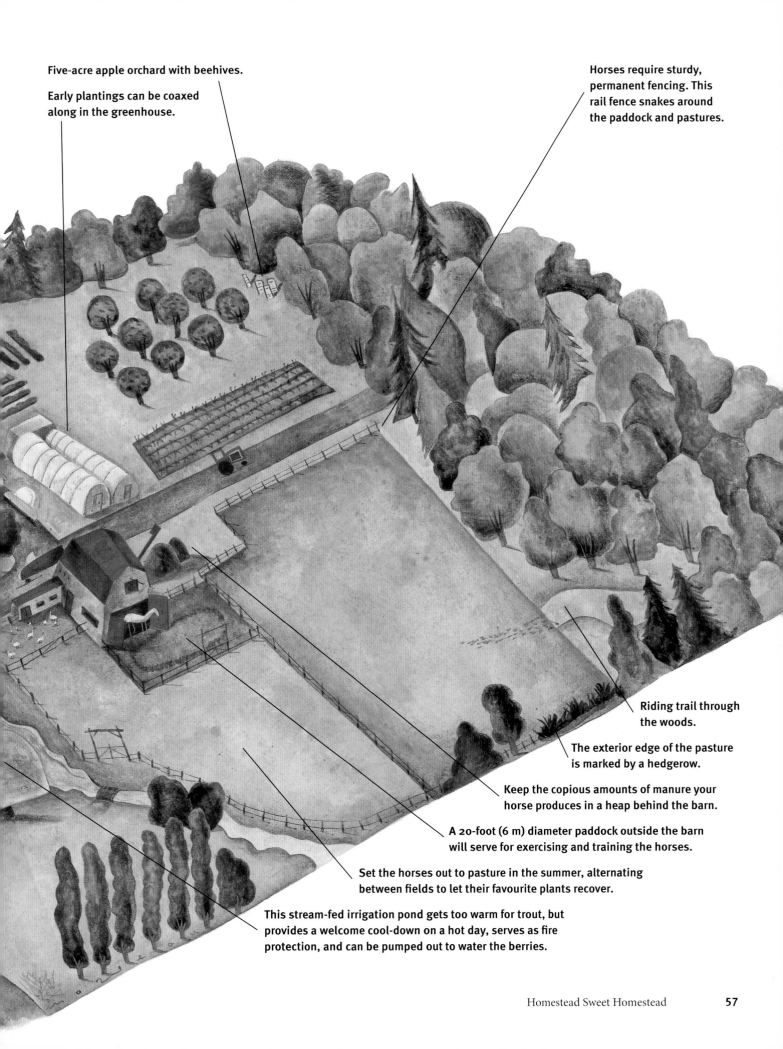

Five-acre apple orchard with beehives.

Early plantings can be coaxed along in the greenhouse.

Horses require sturdy, permanent fencing. This rail fence snakes around the paddock and pastures.

Riding trail through the woods.

The exterior edge of the pasture is marked by a hedgerow.

Keep the copious amounts of manure your horse produces in a heap behind the barn.

A 20-foot (6 m) diameter paddock outside the barn will serve for exercising and training the horses.

Set the horses out to pasture in the summer, alternating between fields to let their favourite plants recover.

This stream-fed irrigation pond gets too warm for trout, but provides a welcome cool-down on a hot day, serves as fire protection, and can be pumped out to water the berries.

Farm Living Is the Life for Me: 35 Acres and Up

Woodlot and Grazing Animals

WITH 35 ACRES or more, Bob's your uncle when it comes to a diversified farm operation. The easiest option is to devote at least a third of the acreage to a woodlot and another third to livestock pasture. Twelve acres, divided into four large fields, would be enough land for 15 to 25 sheep or 7 to 12 grazing beef cattle. Keeping the animals on even smaller parcels of land would enable you to manage the pastures more efficiently by forcing the animals to munch on their second- and third-favourite plants before they move on to a fresh field.

In some folks' opinion, you can't have too much forest. But as a rough minimum, you'll need 10 to 15 acres of woodlot to supply your own firewood throughout most of snow-bound Canada—less in warmer areas. This size of woodlot will provide a perpetual supply if you practise selective thinning. Don't fell majestic hardwoods, just remove broken or dying trees, and those growing too close together. Don't necessarily shun the softwoods—you can burn anything but gummy pine in a woodstove. Even poor-heating woods like cedar and poplar will do for spring and fall, when intense heat is not of the essence.

The sustainable approach to woodlot management allows you to depend on it for all your firewood as long as you might live. But the advantages of a wooded acreage extend further than self-sufficiency and liberation from unpredictable OPEC prices. For one thing, once an immature mixed forest has evolved into a stand of valuable hardwoods, individual maples and oaks can be sold at a handsome profit to a sawmill—again, with selective thinning. And if you're lucky enough to have a stand of sugar maples, small-scale syrup production may be an interesting venture.

The orchard can take up as many acres as you wish, but keep in mind that spraying, pruning and mowing throughout the summer months can be very time-consuming.

A shed for a tractor and other farm machinery is needed to manage a farm of this size.

Extensive lawns lead the eye from the main road to the farmhouse.

A securely fenced barnyard will keep sheep at hand for vaccinations and other special occasions.

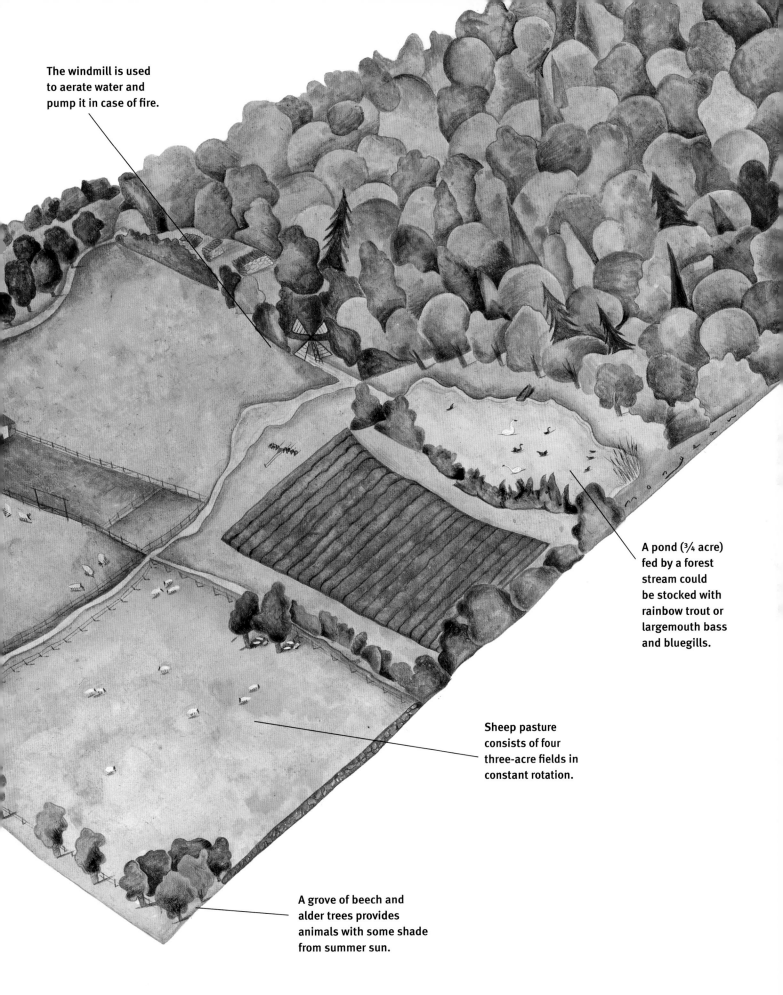

The windmill is used to aerate water and pump it in case of fire.

A pond (¾ acre) fed by a forest stream could be stocked with rainbow trout or largemouth bass and bluegills.

Sheep pasture consists of four three-acre fields in constant rotation.

A grove of beech and alder trees provides animals with some shade from summer sun.

Plotting with Mother Nature

by Carol Hall

ONE OF THE most effective ways to avoid losing vegetable crops to bugs, blights, wilts and other problems is deceptively simple: rotate your crops. But how?

It sounds deceptively easy: Just don't plant vegetables of the same type in the same patch of soil for at least three years. However, what happens when you grow anywhere from 20 to 40 different kinds of vegetables every year? Each has its own soil preference, cultural needs, space requirements and crop-specific pests and diseases that you need to keep in mind. Planning a workable vegetable garden rotation can become a logistical nightmare.

Grouping vegetables with similar needs together, such as peppers, tomatoes and eggplants, makes it easier when planning a crop rotation strategy.

It doesn't have to be. In the 30 years my husband and I have been growing our own vegetables here in coastal British Columbia, we've planned, plotted, changed, revamped, altered, modified, adjusted and readjusted our rotation many times over. We've finally come up with a plan that accommodates the needs of our vegetables, our soil and ourselves all at the same time.

THE BENEFITS OF crop rotation are well proven. For one thing, rotation disrupts the life cycle of disease organisms and insects by relocating their favourite host plants to a new spot every year, which makes it harder for the bugs to find their victims. The brassicas (members of the cabbage family, including broccoli, cauliflower, kale and the like) absolutely require rotation to avoid club root and a host of other maladies. Potatoes, tomatoes, eggplants and peppers (members of the nightshade family) likewise need to be rotated to avoid "catching" serious wilts and blights from bacteria that overwinter in the soil. Similarly, root crops should alternate with leafy crops to short-circuit the dynastic plans of such common pests as root maggots and leaf miners.

Crop rotation also helps keep the soil naturally productive, by preventing the ongoing depletion of nutrients that happens when you plant the same thing in the same spot year after year. Heavy feeders such as corn and melons take a toll on soil fertility, so should be rotated with lighter feeders. In anticipation of corn, we plant peas and beans—legumes that actually add nitrogen to the soil—the year before.

Winter cover crops such as fall rye are another important part of any rotation, since they add valuable nutrients and organic matter to the soil when they're turned under in spring. But since some long-season crops aren't harvested until it's too late to plant fall rye, and others need planting in earliest spring before the turned-under rye has had a chance to decompose, trying to work cover crops into the rotation can get complicated. We've decided to plant fall rye in the final plot, after harvesting its beans, tomatoes, corn, cucumbers and other warm-weather crops. It gets tilled in before planting Plot A (brassicas) the next spring.

Then there's the matter of lime. Magnesium-containing dolomite lime, the type most beneficial to plants, is also one of the slowest acting. This means the soil for lime-loving plants, like brassicas, really should be amended the previous fall—but only if you have the foresight to know where you were going to plant

Lettuce, legumes and some other cool-weather vegetables fall into the "Plot C" category.

them. Liming the whole garden is no solution, since some crops do best without lime (fresh lime will make potatoes scabby, and some plants prefer slightly to moderately acid soil). We lime our garden a quadrant at a time, at the same time and in the same place as we sow winter rye: in Plot D, after the harvest.

OUR PLAN TAKES care of some major complications, but when you tackle crop rotation, many more wrinkles come up. Where do the needs of gardeners fit in, for one thing? And, with eight to ten weeks between cool-weather plantings (peas, onions, potatoes) and warm-weather plantings (squash, peppers, melons), how do you work planting times into the rotation? What about harvest times? Since radishes mature in 25 days or less, while winter leeks and Brussels sprouts can take over 120 days, how do you accommodate succession planting? What about just plain convenience, like having your salad crops grouped in one area and your winter-storage crops in another? And, if you do somehow manage to meet all these conflicting needs this year, what do you do next year, when every crop shifts place again?

Don't despair. The fine-tuning of your crop rotation plan will come with time, as ours did. Gardening is a process of discovery. And one of the first things we discovered was counterintuitive: instead of the three-year rotation usually recommended, a four-year rotation is easier to keep track of, better suited to crop space requirements, and much more practical for grouping crops with similar planting times and/or harvest times. It also makes it easier to custom-amend the soil in fall for the crops that will be planted there come spring.

The details are all spelled out in the chart on page 66, but the basic idea is to divide the garden area into four quadrants and group your veggies into four plots according to their needs for soil fertility and acidity. We start the first plot off right, with added lime, manure and green manure, and as those first, heavy-feeding veggies grow, they use up nutrients and affect pH in such a way as to naturally create the soil conditions preferred by the plot that will follow—and so it goes for the remaining two plots, too.

Our rotation plan succeeds by working with nature, not by fighting against it. And that's the best plan of all.

A · D · B · C

Carol Hall's Crop Rotation Plan

Start with Plot A in the top left, Plot B in the bottom left, Plot C in the bottom right, and Plot D in the top right corner. Then, come planting time next year, rotate the plots clockwise one stop. It will take four years before each crop returns to its original spot on the quadrant, ample time to foil soil-borne diseases or over-wintering insects, and to allow soil nutrients to balance out.

Plot A

Brassicas (Cabbage Family)

CROPS: Broccoli, Brussels sprouts, cabbage, Chinese cabbage, cauliflower, collards, kale, kohlrabi.

NEEDS: These heavy feeders need a deep, fertile, nearly neutral soil (pH around 6.8–7.0).

PREPARATION: After harvesting Plot D last fall (this year's Plot A), you will have dug in a generous layer of manure, planted fall rye and spread dolomite lime. Over winter, the lime has been washed in deeply.

Turn under the rye as early as the ground can be worked.

PLANTING: Transplant early crops about three weeks after turning under fall rye. Plant mid-season and late crops (seeds or transplants) from April to June. Late-season storage crops are best as transplants in late May/early June.

HARVEST: Crops are harvested as they mature (some give repeat harvests). Late crops can be mulched for fall/winter harvest.

Plot B

Root Crops

CROPS: Carrots, parsnips, potatoes, salsify, Swede turnips (rutabagas), winter beets, winter radishes (Asian types).

NEEDS: Fertile soil, not too alkaline (pH around 6.5); high in phosphorus and potassium but not in nitrogen. No fresh manure (causes hairy roots) or lime (causes potato scab).

PREPARATION: Soil is left reasonably fertile but somewhat depleted in lime by Plot A. Extra phosphorus (bone meal or rock phosphate) and potassium (greens and or kelp meal) can be added at planting time.

PLANTING: All crops can be planted early, mid-season and/or late.

HARVEST: In well-drained soil, late crops can be mulched heavily and stored right in the ground until late fall (or all winter in mild climates).

NOTE: Always plant potatoes at one end of the plot; tomatoes, eggplants and peppers at the opposite end of their plot (Plot D), to prevent these nightshade-family crops from revisiting the same soil before four years have passed and thus avoid soil-borne diseases.

Plot C

Legumes, Cool-Weather Crops and Salad Crops

CROPS: Broad beans, green beans, lima beans, peas, celery, green onions, leeks, lettuce/salad greens, spinach, summer beets, summer (bunching) radishes, summer turnips, storage onions, Swiss chard.

NEEDS: Legumes (peas and beans) adapt to any soil type and need little or no extra fertilizer as long as soil is high in organic matter. Except for lettuce, all other crops need or tolerate moderately acidic soil (pH 6.0–65). Most need only moderately fertile soil; onions, leeks and leafy crops need extra nitrogen.

PREPARATION: Soil is left moderately acidic and moderately fertile after Plot B. Turning under the straw or hay used for its winter mulch adds organic matter. Extra nitrogen for onions, leeks and leafy crops can be added at planting time, as can extra lime (if necessary) for lettuce.

PLANTING: All crops except green beans and lima beans (both warm-weather crops) can be planted as soon as the ground can be worked. Salad crops can also be sown in succession or to follow very early crops (broad beans, peas).

HARVEST: Most are repeat-harvesters. Leeks, Swiss chard and succession-sown salad crops can produce well into the frosty period. At summer's end, turn plot over (leaving a corner for fall-producing crops if desired), plant fall rye and lime lightly.

Plot D

Warm-Weather Crops

CROPS: Corn, cucumbers, eggplants, melons, peppers, pumpkins, squashes, tomatoes, zucchini.

NEEDS: Fertile soil, especially at surface; adequate lime (pH around 6.5).

PREPARATION: Soil has been replenished by the legumes from Plot C and the turned-under rye. Lime applied last fall ensures a pH level acceptable to all crops, although lime-tolerant peppers may appreciate more. Compost or aged manure can be dug in at planting time or applied as a top-dressing.

PLANTING: All crops should be planted only after all danger of frost is past and the ground is warm. Melons need consistently warm soil; planting of peppers and eggplants should be delayed until temperatures are above 10°C at night.

HARVEST: Crops are harvested as they mature, but since all are frost tender, harvest is complete by first frost. This leaves plenty of time to dig in manure, plant fall rye and spread dolomite lime in preparation for the brassica crops that will once again occupy the soil as Plot A in spring.

NOTE: Always plant tomatoes, eggplants and peppers on one end of the plot; potatoes at the opposite end of their plot (Plot B), to prevent these nightshade-family crops from revisiting the same soil before four years have passed and thus avoid soil-borne diseases.

A Little Fine-Tuning

THE QUADRANT plan works in theory, but in practice, it might need a little fine-tuning. For instance, leeks are ideally placed in Plot C with other cool-weather crops, but because we like to leave ours in the ground all winter, we plant leeks in Plot A. along with kale and other veggies that keep all winter. This also leaves us more room in Plot C, which we desperately need. Over the years, we've tinkered with the plan and have learned that if space is short in one quadrant, chances are there's room in another.

Crop	Ideal Quadrant	Alternative Quadrant
Beans (green, lima)	C	D
Beets, summer	C	
Beets, winter	B	A
Broad (fava) beans	C	
Broccoli	A	
Brussels sprouts	A	
Cabbage	A	
Cantaloupe	D	
Carrots	B	C
Cauliflower	A	
Celery	C	A
Chinese cabbage	A	
Collards	A	
Corn	D	
Cucumber	D	C
Eggplant*	D	
Endive	C	
Garlic	own permanent bed	C
Herbs, annual	C	D
Kale	A	
Kohlrabi	A	
Leeks	C	A
Lettuce	C	
Melons	D	
Mesclun mix	C	
Mustard	C	
Onions, green	C	
Onions, storage	C	own permanent bed
Parsley	C	perennial herb bed
Parsnips	B	
Peas	C	
Peppers*	D	
Potatoes*	B	
Pumpkins	D	
Radish, summer	C	
Radish winter (Oriental)	B	
Salsify	B	
Spinach	C	
Squash, summer	D	C
Squash, winter	D	
Swiss chard	C	A
Tomatoes*	D	
Turnips, summer	C	
Turnips, Swede (Rutabagas)	B	A
Watermelon	D	

*To avoid soil-borne diseases, no member of the nightshade family—potatoes, tomatoes, eggplants or peppers—should occupy the same soil for at least three years. A foolproof way to keep them separated throughout the four-year rotation, even though they belong to different plots, is this: Always plant potatoes (Plot B) on the same end of their plot (e.g. north, east, closest to the house), and tomatoes/ eggplants/peppers (Plot D) always on the opposite end of theirs (e.g. south, west, farthest from the house).

DAN NEEDLES

A Public Life

True confessions from the Ninth Concession

THERE ARE SOME drawbacks to living in a place where everybody knows your name. Above all, you have to get used to the idea of living in a glass house. Whenever a truck turns down the Ninth Concession to deliver a piece of furniture, or you nip out in your dressing gown to drive the kids to the bus, you know that windows are probably steaming up along the sideroad. Your life is a matter of public record.

I went into the local hospital recently for a routine colonoscopy, something which I had hoped might remain a private matter between the surgeon and me. It turned out that all the nurses working around him could have formed a quorum for the Parents Council at my kids' public school. It reminded me of one of those recurring bad dreams I have where I'm standing in front of an audience without any clothes on. The only difference was that this was really happening.

"Will we be reading about this in *Harrowsmith*?" laughed one of the nurses, who also happens to be my wife's second cousin. "Why not?" I thought. I have spun my web out of thinner thread than this.

I suppose that in some ways, life in the country has changed very little over the years. In the days when small family farms lined the concession roads, everyone lived and worked in full view of their neighbours. Each family followed the same schedule of morning and evening chores and all entered the same race against time and weather to plant and harvest the crops. It was a matter of public record when the lights when on in your barn in the morning, how well you maintained fences, and how successfully you stored up hay and grain to carry your animals through six months of hard winter. A man was judged by the straightness of his furrow and a woman by her skill in the garden and kitchen.

Many of the community's sons and daughters took the first bus south to escape the harsh glare of publicity on the sideroads and re-shape their own destinies. They were rewarded with better-paying jobs in the city and relative anonymity. But they left behind their community—people who, for all their fault-finding, knew them better than anyone else.

Today, many of those wanderers and their descendants are finding their way back to our old rural communities. If their experience is anything like mine, they are probably wondering how much privacy you are expected to give up in exchange for a sense of neighbourhood and belonging.

It's a difficult question and one that bothers even the older residents. They will tell you that the eyes of the neighbours served for more than a century as a pretty effective form of regulation of human behaviour in this township; in fact, they were probably a lot more effective than the parade of government-sponsored busybodies and do-gooders who now invade every nook and cranny in our lives.

I have an old dairy farmer friend who was grumping to me about all the boards, agencies and commissions he reports to and the army of officials who supervise his daily activities. "There's the Milk Marketing Board, the conservation authority, the Niagara Escarpment Commission, the township bylaw enforcement officer, building inspectors, traffic cops, truck cops." He ran down the list shaking his head. "And they still say I need a wife to keep me in line!"

It's true, the neighbourhood telegraph does occasionally suffer an intelligence failure, like the CIA in Iraq. But more often than not, it gets it spectacularly right. Lost dogs and cows are restored promptly to their owners. Storm warnings are issued, houses are checked, meals are delivered to shut-ins and wandering children are herded home safely. And pity the poor man who thinks he can toss a mattress in the ditch out here on the sideroad without being noticed.

For those who are worried about the destructive effects of Rumour and Hearsay, the solution, of course, is to lead an entirely blameless life. Either that, or develop a thicker skin.

> "Will we be reading about this in *Harrowsmith*?" laughed one of the nurses, who also happens to be my wife's second cousin.

Plump radishes and fresh spring onions are among the vegetables delivered to shareholders' doors.

GRACE BUTLAND

Share and Share Alike

Local produce straight from the farm

ANN DWIRE OF Halifax loves the ritual of opening the 50-litre tote box that contains her weekly share of produce from Pumpkin Ecological Farm of West Dalhousie, Nova Scotia. She never knows exactly what she'll find inside, but it's always fresh and it's always organic: potatoes, yellow and green beans, carrots, beets, zucchini, lettuce, peppers and herbs. And that's only a taste of things to come as the growing season reaches its peak.

Ann is one of a growing number of Canadians who have become shareholders in "community shared agriculture" (CSA) farms. In effect, they buy a stake in a farm and reap the dividends not in cash, but in fresh produce. It's a relatively new concept but it is definitely an idea whose time has come.

CSAs first emerged in Japan in the early 1960s, when a group of women who were concerned about the demise of local agriculture and the rise of food imports arranged to purchase directly from nearby farms. The Japanese term for this—*teikei*—means "putting the farmer's face on food." The concept arrived in Canada in 1989, and there are now over 100 CSAs spread across the country.

CSAs help close the gap between farmer and consumer. "It's so easy to become removed from where your food is coming from," says Ann. "CSAs let you re-establish that connection." Consumers buy "shares" in the farm's production and receive a proportionate allotment of the season's crop. They also share in the risks—if rabbits eat all the lettuce, or potato blight hits the crop, shares will be smaller.

The CSA farmer draws up a budget (including overhead such as salaries, seed, tools, distribution, land payments and the like) for the year. The budget, divided by the number of shares that the farm can support, determines the share price. A share will usually supply enough vegetables for a family of four each week for the entire growing season. Most members pay for their shares up front in spring. The cost is greater than in the grocery-store, but usually a little less than shopping at the organic market.

With production costs covered and a guaranteed market for their crops, the farmers are free to concentrate on growing. A typical farm will grow at least 30 kinds of vegetables with as many as four or five varieties of each type. Each week's harvest is divided among the shareholders and delivered to a central distribution point. There is virtually no waste.

Shareholders join for a number of reasons: They like the taste. They prefer organic produce with no chemical additives. They enjoy opening their food box each week and discovering what crops are currently ripe. Many just like knowing where, how and by whom their food is grown.

Most CSAs organize in the spring and operate through the local growing season, usually July through October, though some offer winter shares as well. Most are organic, and some work with other local farmers to include such extras as honey, fruit, eggs and preserves in the shares. Through CSA, Pumpkin Ecological Farm founder Summer North and other farmers across Canada are truly "putting a face on food."

A Taste of Spring

by Darlene King

Cream of Asparagus Soup

Is THERE anything quite as satisfying as a velvety smooth cream soup? Here's a sure-to-please recipe that makes good use of the less-than-showy asparagus stalks if you're saving the tips for something a little more glamorous. However, be sure to reserve a few of the tips as a garnish.

SERVES 6

1 lb	fresh asparagus	450 g
½ cup	water	120 ml
1 Tbsp	butter 15 ml	
¼ cup	onion, chopped	60 ml
½ cup	celery, chopped	120 ml
6 cups	chicken or vegetable stock	1.5 l
3 Tbsp	butter	45 ml
1 cup	35% cream	240 ml
	salt and pepper	
	optional garnish: sour cream, paprika	

Wash and remove the tips from the asparagus. Bring the water to a boil in a small saucepan and simmer for 2 minutes, or until the asparagus is barely tender. Rinse under cold water. Drain and set aside.

Cut the asparagus stalks into 1-inch pieces (2 cm). Set aside

Melt 1 tbsp (15 ml) butter in a large saucepan. Sauté the onion and celery over medium heat until the onion is translucent (about 2 to 3 minutes). Add the uncooked asparagus stalks and the chicken stock. Bring to a boil, reduce heat and simmer for 30 minutes. Remove any scum that comes to the surface.

Remove the pan from the heat and strain the mixture through a sieve, pressing with a wooden spoon to get all the liquid. Reserve the stock.

Melt 3 tbsp (45 ml) of butter in a large saucepan over medium heat. Add the flour and stir until blended. Slowly add the cream, stirring until the soup has thickened. Do not boil. Just before serving, add the reserved asparagus tips to heat through. Adjust salt and pepper to taste.

Garnish each serving with cultured sour cream or a sprinkle of paprika.

Spinach Salad
with Warm Bacon and Maple Walnut Dressing

SERVES 6

6 cups	fresh spinach leaves, stems removed	1.5 l
8	slices bacon, chopped	8
1½ Tbsp	cider vinegar	22 ml
1 Tbsp	maple syrup	15 ml
Salt and freshly ground pepper to taste		
4 Tbsp	bacon drippings	60 ml
⅓ cup	sour cream	80 ml
1	Granny Smith apple, cored and sliced	1
1	Red Delicious apple, cored and sliced	1
¼ cup	raisins	60 ml
¼ cup	walnut pieces, toasted	60 ml

SPINACH SALAD made a big splash in culinary circles in the 1970s and has been a favourite ever since. Here, the old standby is given a whole new twist, thanks to a single subtle spoonful of maple essence.

Wash the spinach thoroughly. Make sure no sand remains on the leaves. Spin or pat dry between paper towels.

Fry the bacon in a medium-sized sauté pan over medium heat until it begins to crisp. Drain on paper towel and set aside. Reserve 4 tbsp (60 ml) of the bacon drippings.

Return the pan with the bacon drippings to the heat. Meanwhile, whisk together the cider vinegar, maple syrup, salt and pepper in a small bowl. Add the mixture slowly to the bacon drippings. Stir well. Remove from heat and let cool slightly before adding the sour cream.

Arrange the spinach on individual serving plates. Fan both types of apple slices over the spinach and sprinkle each plate with bacon pieces, raisins and walnuts. Spoon a little dressing over each of the plates and serve immediately.

Maple Shortbread Cookies

MAKES ABOUT THREE DOZEN TWO-INCH (5 CM) COOKIES.

MAPLE BUTTER

⅔ cup	maple syrup	160 ml
½ cup	butter (room temperature)	120 ml

SHORTBREAD

¾ cup	maple butter	180 ml
2 cups	all-purpose flour	240 ml
¼ tsp	salt	2 ml

THERE'S SOMETHING quintessentially Canadian about this delicious cookie, as it puts a local spin on an old-world tradition. The classic component in traditional Scottish shortbread, whose claim to fame is, of course, the richness of creamery butter. What makes it truly unique is the unmistakable flavour of Canadian maple syrup.

Maple Butter

In a small saucepan, bring maple syrup to a boil and reduce by half, approximately 10 to 15 minutes. Remove from heat and let stand at room temperature. When cool, add the butter and stir until completely blended. Place in refrigerator until firm. Makes ¼ cup (175 ml).

Shortbread

Combine the maple butter, flour and salt in a food processor. Pulse until all the ingredients are well combined and form a ball. Flatten into a disk shape. Wrap in plastic and refrigerate until the dough is well chilled.

Preheat oven to 350°F (175°C). Position rack to centre of oven.

Remove dough from fridge and roll to ¼-inch thickness. Cut dough into desired shapes with cookie cutters. Place cookies on an ungreased cookie sheet and bake until slightly golden-brown, approximately 10 to 15 minutes.

Rhubarb Sour Cream Pie

SERVES 8

PASTRY

1 cup	all-purpose flour	240 ml
2 tsp	sugar	10 ml
½ tsp	salt	2.5 ml
⅓ cup	shortening or lard, chilled	80 ml
1 Tbsp	butter, chilled	15 ml
2 Tbsp	water (more or less)	30 ml

FILLING

4 cups	rhubarb, cut into ½-inch (1.2-cm) pieces	1 l
1½ cups	white sugar	360 ml
⅓ cup	flour	80 ml
1 cup	sour cream	240 ml

TOPPING

½ cup	flour	120 ml
½ cup	brown sugar	120 ml
¼ cup	butter	60 ml

EGG WASH

1	egg yolk	1
3 Tbsp	milk	45 ml

THERE ARE still those among us who claim not to like rhubarb. This tangy sour cream pie, with rhubarb as the star ingredient, is bound to change some minds. Best of all, it's easy to make. The pie can be served at room temperature, but slices better if chilled.

To prepare the pastry

Sift the flour, sugar and salt together into a large bowl. Cut in the shortening and butter with a pastry blender until the mixture is crumbly. Sprinkle with the water and continue blending until all the ingredients hold together. Gather the dough into a ball and flatten into a disc. Wrap in plastic and refrigerate for 30 minutes.

Roll out the pastry dough into a 12-inch (30-cm) circle and transfer the dough to the plate or cookie sheet.

For a rustic presentation, use a flat 9-inch (23-cm) oven-proof plate or bake the pie completely free-form on a cookie sheet.

Preheat the oven to 425°F (220°C).

Topping

Combine ½ cup (120 ml) flour, brown sugar and butter in a bowl. Using your fingertips, rub the mixture together until it forms moist crumbs. Set aside.

Filling

In a medium-sized bowl, mix together the white sugar, ⅓ cup (80 ml) of flour and the sour cream. Set aside. Arrange the rhubarb pieces in the centre of the pie crust, leaving a 3-inch (7.5-cm) border of pastry exposed all around. Spoon the sour cream mixture over the rhubarb. Sprinkle the reserved topping mixture over the sour cream. Fold the crust up toward the centre of the pie and pinch the dough together between you thumb and forefinger to hold the shape.

Egg wash

Combine the egg yolk and milk in a small bowl. Lightly brush the pastry with the mixture. Discard any leftover mixture.

Bake for 15 minutes. Reduce the heat to 350°F (175°C) and continue to bake for 30 minutes longer, or until the pie is a light golden colour.

summer

summer deeds

IF A GARDENER has been diligent in the spring, then summer—particularly late summer—should be a breeze. The compost applied back in May will ensure there is plenty of nourishment for vigorous plants, while heaps of mulch piled on in spring helps the soil retain moisture through a summer drought and smothers any emerging weeds. No fertilizer. No—or at least, fewer—watering chores. No weeds. With techniques like these at hand, a gardener doesn't have much to do come July except admire an alluring display of perennials and set the table for a spectacular harvest of vegetables.

Compost and mulch are often considered the secret weapons of a successful gardener, but more importantly, they are cornerstones in the organic ethic, that method of cultivation that eschews chemical fertilizers and toxic pesticides and herbicides in favour of a more natural approach. Today, this is the fastest growing aspect of the gardening hobby—indeed, organic methods are burgeoning in the commercial agriculture sector, too—but they are really nothing new. Truth to tell, the traditional family farm was an exercise in organics and it's only in the post-World War II era that farming and gardening veered onto a more industrial course. Never one to follow the mainstream, *Harrowsmith* has embraced organic gardening since its inception in 1976.

Thirty years ago, however, the motivation was not what you might expect. Although it's common knowledge now that conventional gardening squanders resources, and there is genuine concern over the lingering residues of chemical fertilizers and pesticides, back then our motivation was to save money. "Prices are never going to go down," read an early editorial, referring to the cost of supermarket produce, "not with the corporate agriculture we're starting to see today." It concluded, "For less then $20 in seed and young plants, you can produce more than $500 worth of vegetables."

In the last three decades, gardening has emerged as one of the growth hobbies, especially among people of a certain age, namely the baby boomers, who long ago traded in their platform heels and designer jeans for wellingtons and a gardener's apron. Along with birdwatching and golf, gardening has become one of the most popular pastimes in the nation and among country people, it is probably the leisure activity of choice, bar none. A country garden is different than its city cousin: Less confined by the dimensions of an urban lot, it is larger and has the chance to meander. By nature, it is also less formal, inviting the visitor to stroll at leisure and take in the sights and scents. But the most significant difference is the extent to which country dwellers grow vegetables. One survey noted that fully 75 percent of rural gardeners devote at least a small plot to tomatoes, potatoes, beans and other staples. One taste of homegrown, organic produce, and you'll know why.

Summer is the season when the garden is at its peak. But if you've done your job right, you'll still have plenty of time for other pursuits: lounging on the verandah, raising sheep, watching the stars. Who'd have thought compost and mulch had such far-reaching benefits?

Eyes Wide Open

by Tom Cruickshank

SOONER OR LATER—perhaps while staring out the window during yet another unfulfilling day at the office—the light dawns on everyone who has ever toyed with the idea of renovating a country house. "Why not open our doors as a bed and breakfast?" After all, with the extra income it generates, it's easier to justify the thousands of dollars that farmhouse renovations often require.

Or is it?

Just ask Bill and Mary Kendrick, B & B hosts on the south shore of Prince Edward Island near the crossroads hamlet of Bedeque. In 2001, they bought a tired farmhouse that was approaching its 90th birthday. At the end of one of PEI's signature red-dirt roads, with a view over one of PEI's quintessential ocean vistas, the three-acre setting was long on charm, an open invitation for guests eager for a walk on the beach and a taste of Maritime hospitality. But the house was another story.

Briarcliffe Inn stands renovated and restored on PEI's south shore. It now boasts five guest rooms.

This bed and breakfast is attractively decorated and stocked with plenty of conversation pieces. It didn't always look as nice as this.

Vacant for five years, it had been neglected too long and would require extensive renovations just to make it habitable, let alone bring the aging dwelling up to the standards of a discerning bed and breakfast. Nevertheless, Bill and Mary were smitten. "We had had a B & B in the backs of our minds for a long time, but figured it would be a project for our 60s," Mary says. And even though it was a little off the beaten tourist path, the house and setting made them think twice about their timing. Very quickly, the empty-nest Kendricks decided that a B & B would be a project for their 50s.

As Bill and Mary Kendrick were contemplating a name for their new bed-and-breakfast establishment, they learned that they weren't the first to open their very same doors to paying guests. For 40 years, until the 1950s, the original owner, Frederica "Fed" MacFarlane had operated the house as the "Briarcliffe Tourist Home." It was only natural to resurrect the old name, and so the Kendricks called their venture the "Briarcliffe Inn."

Despite the romance of their venture, the couple approached their new acquisition with eyes wide open. "The house was structurally sound, but..." Bill says, his voice trailing off. "There were several 'buts.'" Indeed, few of the basic household amenities were operable—neither the hot water tank nor the water softener worked and the two furnaces had long since breathed their last. Water pressure was hopeless for family living, let alone a house full of guests. Meanwhile, the wind whistled through the leaky windows, the sump pump had failed and the plumbing was antiquated. And it was definitely time for a decorative update. "This would have been enough to dampen anyone's enthusiasm," Bill says. But as veterans of several previous renos and housebuilding projects, the couple figured they were up for the job.

Much of the work would have been done regardless—insulation, refinishing the plank floors, peeling away acres of tired wallpaper in preparation for new decor and a hundred other jobs. However, many of the upgrades were specific to a B & B, starting with the number and arrangement of bathrooms. "Some B & Bs merely offer shared baths," Mary explains, "but we had our sights on something more upscale and decided early on that each guest room would have its own." But that's easier said than done in a house that seemed to offer no surplus space. "So, we accommodated new baths in what used to be closets and stole a bit more

BONUS! As an independent television producer, Bill decided to turn their project into a one-hour TV special. "Bed and Breakfast Dream" pops up occasionally on HGTV. Not only did the program allow him to mix business and pleasure, Bill actively recruited sponsors, whose products were incorporated into the footage. He figures the sponsorships shaved $30,000 from their decorating budget.

space from adjoining rooms." Then, to compensate for the loss of storage space, new, smaller corner closets—just ample enough to hang a coat or two—were built. And again in a nod toward pampering guests, the bathrooms were appointed with stylish, luxury fixtures. "No doubt about it, building the bathrooms ate up a disproportionately large chunk of our B & B budget…perhaps adding as much as 50 percent to the total," says Mary.

Providing heat to the guest rooms—all on the second floor—was also a bigger factor than it might otherwise have been. "Like so many farmhouses of its time, heat for the bedrooms was next to non-existent, with one lone register to serve the entire upstairs," Mary observes. In another household, the logical answer might have been to extend the capacity of the forced-air system upward by fishing new ductwork behind the fireplace, closets and other cavities within the walls. "But any available space had already been gobbled up by the labyrinth of additional plumbing, so there was no room left over for ducting," Bill explains. Hence, the Kendricks opted for electric heat, despite its expensive reputation. "It wouldn't have been our first choice, but the electric baseboards also solved another issue: They give guests the ability to control their own heat, which—believe it or not—is a significant point in separating an exclusive B & B from the ordinary."

Although the individually controlled heaters might seem like an unnecessary indulgence, they—and any number of other improvements—were hardly a whim and, in fact, were quite deliberate. "People judge B & Bs on their star rating," explains Mary, referring to the Canada Select Accommodation Rating Program, an industry-run set of standards for bed and breakfasts and hotels across the country. "The more creature comforts there are, the higher the star rating." Indeed, the difference between a three-star and a four-star B & B lies in such amenities as blackout shades, quality furnishings, private baths and yes, individually controlled heat. Even the thread count in the bed linens is a factor. "Certainly, these add to the cost of opening a B & B, but they also offer value for the consumer that justifies a better price for the innkeeper."

The Kendricks not only had appointed their B & B with lots of creature comforts and decorative charm, but they also went beyond the call of duty by actually spending a night in each room. "We 'test drove' every room," Mary says, "to make sure

The butler's pantry was adapted for use as a galley kitchen.

Each lovingly-appointed guest bedroom offers a private bath along with baseboard heating that guests can control themselves.

amenities were well placed, to see where the morning light fell, and to see how noise travels."

For their efforts, the Kendricks earned four-and-a-half stars. "For five stars, we would have had to offer air conditioning, televisions and whirlpool tubs in each room, for which there was simply no room nor budget."

But as they contemplated the renovations, Bill and Mary had more on their minds than their star rating. The couple was working to a deadline that would not have been a factor in an ordinary renovation. They took possession in October, which gave them nine months to render the place guest-worthy in time for the coming tourist season. "That sounds like long enough," confesses Mary, "but considering how much work lay ahead—and that we were going to do much of it ourselves—we were facing a daunting schedule." To get the job done, the couple put their careers on hold—Bill, a TV-news and documentary producer, pared his workload to a bare minimum, while Mary put her antiques business on hiatus. Working 18-hour days, they scraped and stripped, primed and painted. Meanwhile, they put the squeeze on contractors and recruited family, friends and any other able body willing to get in on the act. By Christmas, the house was at least habitable enough to allow the couple to move in. And by June 15, 2002, the finishing touches were, by and large, completed. "We were lucky," says Bill, "because our first guests were booked for June 17."

A SIGNIFICANT PORTION OF renovation costs lies in basic services and technical upgrades that can't be seen. For example, the Kendricks' septic system has twice the capacity of a normal household's. Likewise, good water pressure is crucial, as there might be five people taking a shower at any time. The couple even bought a $1,000 generator in case of a power blackout.

The project went about $20,000 over budget, thanks largely to a couple of unwelcome surprises. "As our contractor was getting ready to install our new deck, he discovered that the main sill (the structural component on which the weight of the entire house rests) was rotten and in dire need of repair," explains Mary. "And then he uncovered a nasty leak over the bay window that had gone unchecked for years."

Undaunted, the Kendricks never looked back, and in fact, embarked on new projects that expanded their capacity from the original three guest rooms to five. "We turned the attic into our most luxurious guest suite," explains Bill, and most ambitious of all, he and Mary renovated what was the summer kitchen into their own private quarters. Not only does this free up their former bedroom for use as a guest room, but it also allows a measure of privacy between guests and hosts. "A good host soon learns that a certain amount of separation is a good thing," says Mary. And it seems this wasn't the only lesson she and Bill learned, for by 2006, the Kendricks were turning a profit.

The fact that the Kendricks turned a profit so soon was no fluke. "We interviewed 20 B & B hosts before taking the plunge," Mary says, "and they all said the same thing. Don't take on more than you can handle."

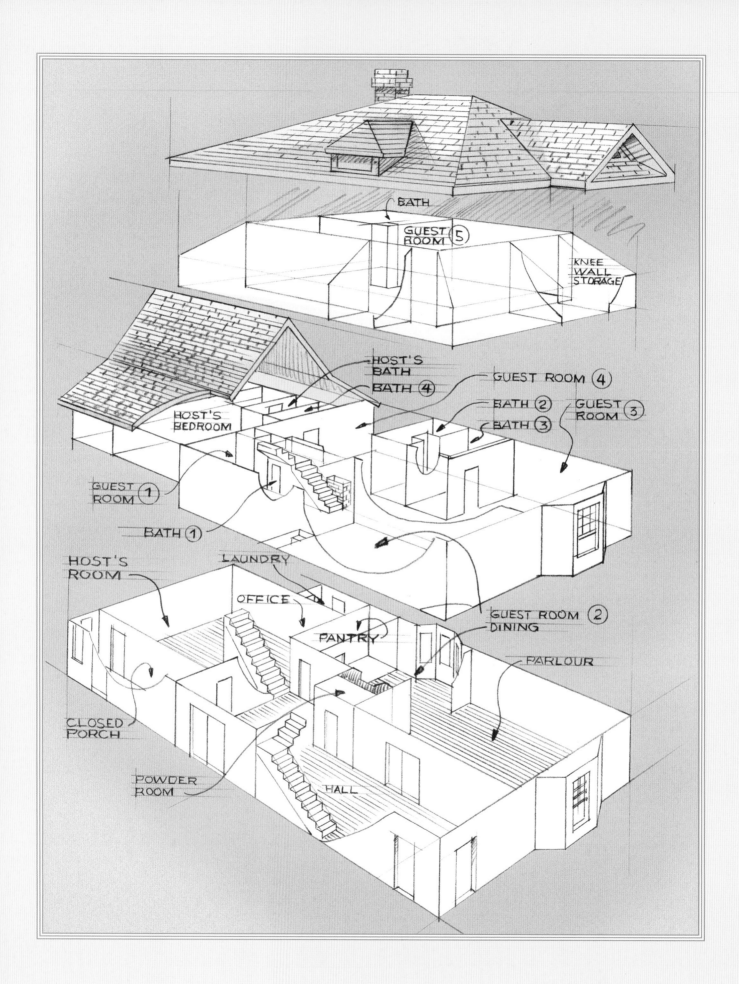

BATH

GUEST ROOM 5

KNEE WALL STORAGE

HOST'S BATH

BATH 4

GUEST ROOM 4

BATH 2

BATH 3

GUEST ROOM 3

HOST'S BEDROOM

GUEST ROOM 1

BATH 1

HOST'S ROOM

LAUNDRY

OFFICE

PANTRY

GUEST ROOM 2

DINING

PARLOUR

CLOSED PORCH

POWDER ROOM

HALL

Specs

CONCEPT: Two-storey Edwardian-era farmhouse with usable attic. Renovated and adapted to function as a bed-and-breakfast establishment. Owners acted as their own general contractor. Primary consultant: Darrell McHugh, Schurman Construction, Summerside, PEI.

GENESIS: Purchased October 2001; occupied Christmas 2001 with three guest rooms. Summer kitchen tail adapted as hosts' private quarters and guest accommodation expanded to five rooms in spring of 2004.

LOCATION: On Salutation Cove on the south shore of Prince Edward Island.

BEDROOMS: 5 plus host's suite.

BATHROOMS: 5 plus ground-floor powder room and host's bath.

TOTAL USABLE FLOOR AREA: about 3,600 square feet on three levels, including host's quarters in former summer kitchen tail.

CONSTRUCTION: Typical wood-frame structure on fieldstone foundation.

CLADDING: Shingle siding in typical Maritime fashion.

ROOF: Asphalt shingles.

WATER AND SEPTIC: Existing well collapsed during repair, so a new one was drilled to 105 feet with submersible pump; conventional septic system with extra-large tank (to accommodate extra water demand by guests).

HEAT: Central oil-fired furnace with conventional forced-air ductwork. Upstairs guest rooms heated by individually controlled electric baseboard units.

INSULATION: Blown cellulose (walls); fibreglass batts (attic ceiling).

ELECTRICAL: service Standard 200-amp service .

WINDOWS: New double-glazed sash-operated thermal units.

Love Among the Ruins

A *Harrowsmith Country Life* Staff Report

I T WAS EITHER knock it down, or let it fall down," say Georg and Karen Maier, recalling their decision over the fate of the weathered old barn that stood adjacent to their century stone house near Durham, Ontario. After years of neglect, it needed thousands of dollars of structural repairs to make it usable, but it was an expense the Maiers just couldn't justify. "We are avid country dwellers, but we aren't farmers, and had no real use for such a big barn." So down it came. A crane and crew were on hand for four days to dismantle it, and salvageable timbers were given to the farmer next door to build a new shed. It took another two years of Saturdays to clean up the mountain of manure and debris left behind. Finally, all that remained were the cement silo, stone foundation walls and the concrete floor.

When the barn came down, the garden went in.
The pond and a host of irises bask in the sunlight.

After removing the concrete flooring in the former barn, Karen and Georg blended a mix of rotted manure, compost and topsoil to provide fertile soil for growing their favourite perennials.

FOR ANOTHER COUPLE, the story might have ended there, but for Karen and Georg, it marked the beginning of an unlikely saga that saw the barn foundation transformed into a garden of unparalleled beauty. No longer the domain of cows and crops, the barn is now the backdrop for an extensive array of ornamental plants. Clematis and hydrangea vines climb the rugged stone walls, while a perennial garden blooms on the very spot where the dairy herd used to be milked. The manure gutters and feeding troughs are now planting beds. A concrete cistern, collapsed into pieces, was left where it fell, like some ancient architectural monument. Even the silo, long empty of feed and not the most likely candidate for greenery, has new life as a grotto, a place for contemplation.

"It's come a long way," Karen says. "At first, converting the foundation into a garden was just an experiment." Little did she and Georg know it would turn into such an exotic and inviting landscape. Soaking up the sun amid the fabulous flora, you can

Adjacent to the house (note the greenhouse addition at the rear), Georg and Karen planted a theme garden in white.

The abandoned silo was a logical spot to create a grotto. Moss grows naturally.

Love Among the Ruins

Plan of Garden

1 **Silo grotto**

2 **Pergola and seating area**

3 **Perennials, including dame's rocket, peony, viola, lamb's ear, sweet William and poppies**

4 **Collapsed cistern**

5 **Shrub roses**

6 **Clematis**

7 **Rugosa roses**

8 **Climbing roses**

9 **Former manure gutter**

10 **Delphiniums**

11 **White veronicas**

12 **Yellow thyme**

13 **Daylilies**

14 **Feeding trough: annuals**

15 **Thyme and groundcovers**

16 **Cherry tree**

17 **Lavender**

18 **Raised bed (squash)**

19 **Low concrete wall**

20 **Perennials, including foxglove, monkshood and hyssop**

21 **Raised bed (artemesia)**

22 **Zebra grass**

23 **Arbour**

24 **Apricot tree**

25 **Cedar hedge**

26 **Pond**

27 **Japanese irises**

28 **Poppies**

29 **Pussy willow**

30 **Weeping willow**

31 **Urns**

32 **Storage**

33 **Juniper edge**

be forgiven if thoughts drift to distant Mediterranean locales.

"Mediterranean" is an apt description, for the barn-foundation garden has an air similar to an ancient Hellenistic ruin, about as far from rural Ontario as you can get. And the comparison goes beyond aesthetics. "The stone walls trap the warmth of the sun," explains Georg. "They actually create a much hotter and drier microclimate than you would expect up here in Zone 5B. Our magnolias grow to a respectable eight feet (2.5 m) and the perennials are still blooming in mid-October, especially along the south-facing walls." No wonder the Maiers like to pretend they're basking on a Greek isle in the Aegean. In fact, there's probably too much sunshine. "We wanted variety in our garden design, so we built a pergola in one corner that would provide filtered shade."

"I DON'T REMEMBER THE precise moment when it occurred to us to turn the barn ruin into a fantasy garden," Georg continues. Before the barn was demolished, the couple had already tried their hand at some foundation planting and liked the visual contrast of the delicate flowers against the rustic stone. "From there, we got the idea for a walled garden." But even when the barn was finally down, Georg and Karen had reservations. Was the scope of the project beyond them? After all, the barn covered 5,000 square feet (465 m²). And then there was the practical problem of how to establish a flower garden on the concrete floor. "We wondered if we'd bitten off more than we could chew."

They needn't have worried, for the barn ruin quickly turned into a labour of love. "No question, it was backbreaking, tedious work," says Georg, remembering the arduous task of preparing the barn ruin for ornamental plants. The hard part, of course, was what to do with the poured-concrete floor. "Much of it had to be removed to make way for the planting beds, but some was retained for patios and walking paths."

Undaunted, Georg simply started by taking a sledgehammer to the floor—in places, it was up to four inches (10 cm) thick—and carving out a pattern of walkways and garden beds. "The job went easier when I rented a masonry saw, and eventually I hired a student to complete the dirty work," he says, recalling his aching back.

Still, the grunt work wasn't finished. "Under the concrete was a thick layer of gravel, which had to be shovelled out by hand," Georg says. And even then, some strenuous hours lay ahead

as the beds were prepared with a one-foot-deep (30 cm) blend of three-quarters rotted manure and one-quarter compost and topsoil. "One thing about gardening in the country—an ample supply of manure is always as handy as the dairy farm next door," says Georg. It was only when the soil was finally mixed that Georg and Karen could turn their attention to planting.

"We took our time and let it evolve," says Karen. "We made some mistakes along the way—we probably underestimated the intensity of the sun, and we found out the hard way that the lower reaches of the barn floor are under water until well into May—but learning is part of the fun of gardening." To this day, the ruin remains a work in progress. "May is our busiest month—planting, tilling the soil, planning new beds. It's not unusual for each of us to spend 15 hours a week gardening, but you know, it never feels like a chore. It's a hobby. An evening in the garden is as good as a holiday."

GEORG IS THE creative brains behind the project. "I love the design phase," he says. "Unlike some of our gardening pursuits, we approached the foundation garden with a plan in mind." Guiding the design were some basic parameters: how best to take advantage of microclimates, and creating different points of interest. "Above all, we wanted to include our favourite colours and perennials—delphiniums, lupins, lilies, poppies, irises, foxgloves and peonies—and lots of climbing vines."

The barn foundation is the most ambitious, but is only one expression of the Maiers' abiding love of gardening. Their property also boasts a white-flower theme garden next to the house, a prolific patch of herbs and more vegetables than they could ever hope to eat. Gardening was also the motivation behind one of their many home improvement schemes: A greenhouse was added to the south side of their house, ensuring that they can indulge their hobby year round. Currently under way are new projects, including an orchard and more planting beds, but it's the barn garden that continues to satisfy them the most. "It was the biggest challenge," Karen muses. "But the rewards make it worth our while."

Once cow stalls, now a conversation corner: The rustic pergola provides filtered shade.

If You Can't Stand the Heat, Get Out of the Kitchen

by Kathryn McHolm

I F YOU WERE a settler making your way to wilderness Canada in the early 19th century, you would probably already have known about our legendary winters. However, you would likely be completely unprepared for summer, which, as we have all since learned, can be nothing short of stifling, especially in the east, where the heat and humidity are more reminiscent of the Everglades than the Great White North.

No wonder the pioneer housewife avoided baking in the summer. No wonder she often took her baking outside to a crudely constructed oven not far from her back door.

Like the smokehouse and the root cellar, the outdoor bakeoven was an important component of the well-equipped homestead. Although the more sophisticated were made of brick or stone, homemade bakeovens could be made of even simpler materials, namely adobe; that is, ordinary sun-dried clay applied to a bent-twig frame.

Kathryn McHolm puts her adobe oven to the ultimate test: Can it make a decent pizza? (Yes, it can.)

If the building materials were rudimentary, so were the cooking techniques: Build a wood fire in the oven till the adobe walls get good and hot; scrape out the coals; and then, by guess and by golly, time the baking just right. Less precise than today's high-tech kitchens perhaps, but the results were worth it—some still say there's nothing better than fresh bread baked in a wood-fired oven.

But before you lament the loss of the traditional bakeoven, read on…for not only can we show you how to make the best wood-fired breads and pizzas, we can even show you how to make the oven to cook them in.

Outdoor Baking: A Brief Canadian History

"At present we bake in a bake-pan, but an oven is one of the things we intend to have next year." So wrote the pioneer author Anne Langton, still known in historical circles for *A Gentlewoman in Upper Canada*, written in the mid-1800s. In documenting the travails of life in the fledgling colony, Miss Langton lamented the lack of luxuries in the backwoods and looked forward to indulging in some of life's conveniences, such as a real oven. Chances are she was referring to a masonry oven to be built as an appendage to the fireplace hearth in her brand new kitchen. She probably would have thought an outdoor oven crude and only occasionally useful.

Still, outdoor ovens persisted in pioneer Canada, especially in Quebec and other French-settled regions. In fact, they were still being used by country folk long after their city cousins had graduated to electric and gas ovens. "Tradition died hard in French Canada," noted one scholar. "If it wasn't broke, nobody bothered to fix it."

Because it could be built from adobe clay, twigs and other materials close at hand, an outdoor bakeoven was integral to the pioneer homestead. And even though every family would eventually graduate to an indoor, masonry oven (and later, a cast-iron, wood-burning cookstove), the homemade type never fell completely from favour. Indeed, outdoor ovens came in handy during the summer months, when the heat from the kitchen hearth could render the entire house unbearably hot. "Like the end of the school year, baking bread outdoors was a ritual of summer at our house," recalls a woman who grew up in the francophone townships of Simcoe County, Ontario. "We couldn't wait for bread day—the aroma was heavenly."

An Adobe Bakeoven

IT'S NOT like you can run down to Canadian Tire and buy an adobe oven. Indeed, traditional outdoor clay ovens—built from earth and other components found in the ground or around the farm—are an all-but-lost art. Still, like quilting, cheesemaking, rug hooking and a handful of other household skills once considered obsolete, there's a growing interest in them. It has something to do with pride in making something yourself … with carrying on a tradition practised for generations … with being self-sufficient. It also has something to do with better-tasting pizza, for the wood-fired oven adds a distinctive accent to anything baked in it.

The cost is next to nothing. The model shown here employs homemade or recycled materials only. However, what you save in materials, you spend in labour. Indeed, this is not a project for the impatient. Construction is a three-day job, and it takes a good two weeks for the work to dry. And then there's the inaugural all-day fire, which vitrifies the clay. Only then is the oven ready for your first pizza. But it'll be worth the wait.

Tools Required

- Shovel
- Chisel and saw
- Thirty-two 3″ screws
- Electric drill or brace and bit
- Spirit level
- Measuring tape
- Carpet tacks
- Ten 2″ nails
- Pails
- Whisk or broom
- Wheelbarrow
- Hammer
- Burlap bags or old blankets
- Four 2″ spikes
- Rasp

Materials List

BASE

- Eight 4 x 4 cedar, 37″ long—for crib base
- Nine 4 x 4 cedar, 32″ long—for crib base
- Eight 4 x 4 cedar, 46″ long—for tabletop
- One 32″ x 37″ sheet aluminum, cut to size. Use recycled material from a scrap dealer or roof flashing.
- Two 1 x 1 wooden battens, 30″ long—for batten frame
- Two 1 x 1 wooden battens, 37″ long—for batten frame. The frame keeps sand from spilling out over the edge of the tabletop.
- 35 9″ x 4½″ x 2½″ firebricks—for oven floor

OVEN

- About twenty 10-litre pails of clay—for walls and dome. This need not be fancy potter's material; roadside or river clay will do just fine. Just ask the landowner before you help yourself.
- About ten 10-litre pails of sand—clay and sand are the basic ingredients in the adobe bricks.
- Pail of water—keep on hand for mixing and making bricks.
- ½ bale of hay or roadside grass—used as a binding agent in the adobe bricks.
- 16 cedar twigs (including eight 49″ long, bent into hoops); the rest can be longer or shorter, left straight. The twigs form the shape of the dome.
- 10 feet of string
- One angle iron, 16″ long—part of the door frame.
- Two metal strips, 12″ long, drilled in two places—part of the door frame.
- Juice can for chimney stopper—an ordinary tin can plugs the chimney hole and helps the oven retain heat.
- 24″ x 24″ (approximately) matte board—for underside of dome roof.
- Scrap lumber, 1½″ thick, enough to fashion a 12″ square door.
- Wooden drawer pull or homemade door handle.

NOTE: All dimensions for the oven shown here are based on standard 9″ x 4 ½″ firebricks, which when laid in place, make the 32″ x 46″ surface (see Step 3). Larger or smaller bricks are certainly acceptable, but be prepared to adjust all other dimensions accordingly. Before final assembly, it might be a good idea to test-fit the parts to ensure that the bricks, tabletop and crib match up nicely.

ANOTHER NOTE: Make sure lots of warm, sunny days lie ahead, as building with adobe is not a cold-weather project. The oven needs about two weeks to dry completely. Frost could cause untimely flaking and cracking.

Day One

STEP 1
Excavation

It is important that the oven rests on a frost-worthy surface—otherwise, it will be unduly prone to cold-weather cracks and seasonal heaves. A simple sand foundation—a 5 feet x 5 feet hole, 36″ deep (to the frost line in your area), backfilled with sand—should suffice.

Day Two

STEP 2
Building the Crib Base

Using a chisel or a saw, cut a 2″ x 4″ notch from each end of the nine 32″ crib-base 4 x 4s. Assemble the crib base, log-cabin style (a). As you progress, secure each member to the one below it with two 3″ screws. Countersink screws when necessary. On the final tier, add an extra cross-member for good measure.

STEP 3
Building the Tabletop

Align the 46″ 4 x 4s atop the crib to form a tabletop (b). If you have measured precisely, only the two members on the outside edges need to be secured to the crib below (c). (Drill a hole halfway through the lumber; then insert a 3″ screw.) The others should wedge into place. Use a spirit level to check that the tabletop surface is level.

Lay the sheet aluminum over the entire tabletop. It acts as a fire barrier. Make sure it lies completely flat. Tack it in place.

Secure the batten frame around the perimeter (d) with 2″ nails.

Pour in sufficient sand to cover the metal surface and fill to the brim of the frame (e). This is the surface on which the bricks will lie, so make sure it is absolutely level.

STEP 4
Laying the Firebricks

Lay firebricks in place. Set them together as closely as possible (f). No mortar is necessary. Brush the joints with sand (g).

STEP 5
Skim Coat

In a bucket, wet 4 cups of clay with water until the mixture is the consistency of whipping cream (h).

Dampen the brick surface and apply a skim coat of clay (i).

Wait 10–15 minutes and repeat to ensure a good coating on the bricks.

Care and Maintenance

- When not in use, protect the oven under a plastic tarpaulin. Better yet, build a wooden canopy to shield it from the elements, just like our ancestors did.
- Don't be alarmed if the surface develops a few hairline cracks over the winter. Small cracks—say, less than ⅛″—can be filled with new clay and worked to a smooth surface.
- Small repairs are easy. Like mending plaster, simply groove out the crack, wet both sides and fill with new clay. Apply damp burlap so that the surface dries gradually.
- After a few years, you may have to apply a new skim coat of clay to the oven floor.

STEP 5 CONT'D.

Note: Do not apply clay to the row of bricks that will function as the shelf (j). Keep surface as smooth as possible.

STEP 6
Scoring the Wall Outline

Before the clay has a chance to dry thoroughly, score the surface to mark the thickness of the perimeter walls (k)—4″. Allow 12″ for a doorway opening.

STEP 7
Making Adobe Bricks

Using 2 pails of clay to 1 pail of sand, slowly add water until you can knead the mixture like bread dough (l). You will be using a lot of clay for the next few steps, so mix it in a wheelbarrow.

Using your hands, shape a dollop of clay into the form of a brick (m), about 8″ long x 4″ wide x 2″ to 3″ thick. As you mould each brick, add a handful of hay, which acts as a binding agent.

STEP 8
Laying the First Brick

Starting at one corner, lay the first brick within the outlines drawn on the tabletop (n). Lay the next brick beside it. Lay the next layer to a height of about 8″. Work your way around the perimeter, filling in gaps with more clay. Work the surface with your hands until it is smooth and shows no joints.

Don't forget to allow a 12″ gap for the doorway opening. Call it a day when the first two rows are finished (o). To keep the row soft and malleable for tomorrow, wrap the clay with damp burlap or a damp blanket. If any clay is left in the wheelbarrow, keep it covered until you return to work.

Day Three

STEP 9
Making the Dome Frame

Shape eight 49″ cedar twigs into hoops and tie their bases together with string. Secure the hoops in place by nudging each end against the inside of wall (p). It's tempting, but do not poke the twigs into the clay.

STEP 10
Building the Adobe Walls

Lay the next layer of bricks. As work proceeds, fill any gaps and smooth out edges with additional clay until no joints are visible. Continue until the second row is done (q). Keep the walls damp—do not let the clay dry out.

Cooking Tips

COOKING IN an adobe oven is an acquired skill. After all, is there any other cooking device that suggests you test the temperature with your arm?

• Build a good fire with kindling and firewood—cedar is a good choice. Make sure chimney-stop and door are not in place. Light the fire and let burn for at least an hour before baking.

• After the fire has died down, stick your arm in the oven to test the temperature. If you can only stand to hold your arm in there for a count of ten or less, the oven is too hot and should cool substantially before you bake anything. If you can do it for a count of 20, it's not hot enough, and you should build the fire up again. At a count of 15, the heat is just about right.

• Two other ways to determine when the temperature is right for baking:
1) A handful of flour tossed into the oven turns golden brown;
2) The dome is white and the embers have cooled to ash.

• Remove the embers with long-handled fireplace tools and let them cool.

• You can bake several items in the oven at the same time. The hard part is manipulating the tools to remove them after baking. Likewise, the temperature of the oven floor will be inconsistent. It will have hot spots and very hot spots—it takes practice to learn the oven's idiosyncrasies.

• Secure the door and chimney stopper in place while baking.

• Sneak a peek now and then to check on progress, but not too often.

STEP 11

Doorway Frame

When the walls reach a height of 12″, it's time to place the doorway frame. First, test the two sides of the doorway opening with a spirit level (r, page 103); then, set the doorway angle iron in place (s). Cover the angle iron with daubs of clay (t).

STEP 12

Dome Construction

Shape the rest of the dome twigs with the rest of the cedar twigs.

Wedge them in place—front to back and criss-cross (u). Keep symmetry in mind as you place them.

When the back wall reaches 15″ high, make a place for the chimney hole. Hold the tin-can chimney stopper in place (v) and pile on the clay bricks until it holds fast. Tomorrow, before the clay is completely dry, twist the chimney stopper loose so that it won't be glued in place permanently.

Continue to add more layers of adobe bricks (w), but before the

dome is closed over, secure the matting board in place (x). It ensures the inside roof of the dome will be a smooth surface. Use it as a base as you wedge the final bricks in place (y).

STEP 13
Doorway Details

Secure the metal strips in the doorway and tap in place (z). Make a door from scrap wood—use thick lumber or two layers. Test fit the door (aa) and, using a rasp or a chisel, whittle it to a precise fit. Fashion a door handle from spare twigs or use a wooden pull. Do not use metal hardware.

Remove the tin-can stopper. Patch any flaws in the chimney hole.

The construction is now complete. Cover the oven with damp burlap and let the oven dry gradually, shaded from the sun. This can take up to two weeks, depending on the weather.

Check the oven surface daily to ensure the clay isn't drying out too quickly. You can speed up the drying of the inside a little by lighting small kindling fires in the oven. If rain is expected, cover the oven with a plastic tarp. When the outside surface appears dry, remove the burlap.

When the work appears to be dry, light a respectable fire inside the dome. Let the cedar hoops and matting board go up in smoke. In fact, keep the fire going all day in order to "vitrify" (a potter's term) the clay. The fire inside may reach as high as 650°F (340°C), so be careful of the heat.

RECIPES BY DARLENE KING

The Stuff of Life

Recipes for your new outdoor adobe oven

These delicious recipes will work just as well in a conventional oven in your kitchen.

Smoked Salmon Pizza

SERVES 4
COOKING TIME 40 MINUTES
PREPARATION TIME 25 MINUTES

½ cup	warm water (105°F or 40°C)	120 ml
2 tsp	olive oil	10 ml
1½ cups	all-purpose flour	360 ml
½ tsp	salt	2.5 ml
1 tsp	fast-rising, active dry yeast	5 ml
2 Tbsp	vegetable oil	30 ml
1	small red onion, sliced thinly	1
¼ tsp	sugar	1.2 ml
1 8-oz	package of herbed cream cheese, softened	250 g
¾ lb	smoked salmon, thinly sliced	300 g
1 Tbsp	dill mustard	15 ml
2 Tbsp	pickled capers, drained	30 ml

OUR ARTICLE on bakeoven cooking would be incomplete without at least one recipe for a genuine wood-oven baked pizza. This is a thin-crust type, which makes one 14″ pizza or two 8″ pizzas. It can be served as you would any pizza, but also makes an inspiring dish for an informal breakfast or brunch.

Add the warm water to the olive oil in a measuring cup.

Combine the flour, salt and yeast in a large bowl. Make a well in the centre of the dry ingredients and pour in the liquid mixture. Stir. Turn the dough out onto a floured surface and knead, adding more flour if necessary. Work until the dough is soft and small bubbles begin to form just under the surface, approximately 7–10 minutes. Generously grease a large bowl, drop in the dough and let rise until doubled in bulk, approximately 1 hour.

While the dough is rising, make the toppings. Warm the vegetable oil in a sauté pan over medium-high heat. Add the onions and sprinkle with the sugar. Reduce the heat to medium. Cook the onion until it has caramelized (turned a medium amber colour). Remove from the heat and cool.

Preheat the oven to 425°F (220°C), or make sure the outdoor bakeoven is ready.

If using a pizza stone or pan, roll out the dough to a circle of approximately 12″–14″ (30–35 cm). Let it rest for five minutes. Place it in the oven and bake for 10–12 minutes or until just beginning to brown.

Remove the crust from the oven to add the toppings. First, spread the cream cheese over the surface. Arrange the salmon slices over the cheese and drizzle with a little of the dill mustard. Place the caramelized onions on top and sprinkle with the capers. Put the pizza back in the oven for 3–5 minutes. Serve immediately.

Granola Wood-Baked Bagels

MAKES 12 BAGELS
PREPARATION TIME 1½ HOURS
COOKING TIME 30 MINUTES

1¼ cups	warm water	240 ml
2 Tbsp	honey	30 ml
1 Tbsp	active dry yeast	15 ml
1 tsp	salt	5 ml
2 Tbsp	vegetable oil	40 ml
2- cups	all-purpose flour	600 ml
½ cup	granola	120 ml
¼ cup	raisins	60 ml
¼ cup	sunflower seeds	60 ml
8 cups	hot water	2 litres
1 Tbsp	sugar	15 ml
½ cup	granola	120 ml
1	egg yolk	1
2 Tbsp	water	30 ml

EVER HAD a Montreal bagel? If you have, you know the secret lies not only in the recipe, but in the technique. Baked in a wood-fired oven, they have a unique taste whose fame has spread well beyond the bagel emporiums of Montreal. Now you can make your own.

Heat the water to 105°F (40°C). Add the honey and stir. Add the yeast and allow it to "proof" (dissolve and become foamy), approximately 7 minutes. Stir lightly.

Combine the yeast mixture, salt and vegetable oil in a bowl. Mix well.

In another bowl, combine 2¼ cups of the flour (reserve the remaining ¼ cup; it will be added gradually as you knead the dough), the first measure of granola, raisins and sunflower seeds. Make a well in the centre of the dry ingredients. Pour in the yeast mixture and stir until the dough holds together in a loose ball.

Turn onto a lightly floured board and knead for 7 minutes, adding more flour as necessary to make the dough firm enough to handle.

Generously grease a large bowl. Place the dough in the bowl, and let it rise until almost doubled in size (1½ to 2 hours).

Punch down the dough and let it rest for a few minutes. Sprinkle flour over a large work surface, and using a rolling pin, roll the dough into a rectangle. Divide into 12 equal pieces.

Using your hands, roll a piece back and forth on your work surface to make a rope approximately 7″ (17 cm) long and tapered at each end. Overlap the ends and join the dough together. Place on a baking sheet lined with baking parchment paper; repeat the process with the rest of the dough pieces. Cover and let the bagels rise for 15 minutes.

Preheat a conventional kitchen oven to 400°F (200°C), or have the outdoor wood-fired bakeoven well stoked.

Meanwhile, back in the kitchen, bring the 8 cups of hot water and sugar to a gentle boil. Three at a time, add the bagels and boil for 20 seconds. Then turn them with a slotted skimmer and continue to boil for 20 seconds more. Remove from the pot and place on a greased baking sheet.

Pour the second measure of granola into a small bowl. Mix the egg yolk with the water and place in a bowl beside the granola. Dip the top half of the bagel in the egg mixture, and then gently press into the granola. Return to the baking sheet. Repeat with the remaining bagels.

Place the bagels in the oven and bake for 20 minutes or until golden brown.

An Heirloom Garden

by Tom Cruickshank

PERHAPS IT'S ONLY natural that two professors of history would find their niche tending a garden inspired by the past. Sure enough, Paul Fritz and David Russo, both retired from the history department of McMaster University in Hamilton, Ontario, gave more than a nod to antiquity when they built the gardens that adorn their farmhouse in eastern Ontario's Rideau Lakes region. Enclosed by traditional dry stone walls and cedar-rail fences, the landscape is awash with special varieties of poppies, peonies and other perennials that were better known in the 19th century than they are today. Likewise, the vegetable patch has a section devoted solely to heirloom varieties quite distinct from modern supermarket fare. And for design advice, they turned to no less than the great gardening gurus of long ago, including the works of William Robinson, Marjery Fish and Gertrude Jekyll; indeed, Paul and David even borrowed some lessons from the ancient Celts.

Dry stone walls divide the garden into "outdoor rooms," each with its own theme.

A rustic gate and gardening tools complement the abundance of old-time perennials.

Things didn't start out that way. When Paul acquired the 40-acre property in 1973, the small stone farmhouse stood forlorn, with hardly a lilac bush to hide its naked foundation. "At the time, gardens were the last thing on my mind," he recalls. "My first priority was to fix up the house." Born and raised in the area, Paul bought the circa 1829 dwelling as a weekend retreat to be closer to family and ancestral roots. "I had known the farm from my childhood—in fact, it was home to five generations of relatives on my mother's side."

Paul also knew that it had hardly been touched over the years. Most of the important architectural details—baseboards,

fireplaces, mantels, floors, hardware and trim—were still in place. So what if it lacked indoor plumbing and running water? For a historian like Paul, this was a dream come true. Over the years, he restored the house to the letter, ensuring that modern upgrades such as kitchen cabinets and bathrooms were placed where they would least distract from the 19th-century ambience. It was the same with exterior appointments. "I wanted the house to look as it would have when it was new, but I also wanted the conveniences of modern life," he says. "It isn't easy, but you can reconcile the two eras." This explains why Paul never paved the driveway, and it is also the reason why he buried the hydro lines.

Taking a lesson from William Hogarth, the extensive perennial border cuts a serpentine swath across the lawn.

THE GARDENS CAME about only ten years ago, almost by accident, and only after the house restoration was largely completed. "We stumbled into gardening when I rescued some specimens from my grandmother's house in the nearby village of Delta," Paul says. The house was about to be sold outside the family, so he helped himself to some souvenirs—spring bulbs, peonies, mock oranges and more—and transplanted them in a formal arrangement beside his farmhouse. "Little did we realize then," adds David, "that many of Paul's grandmother's specimens were actually rare heirloom varieties. Maybe it's because we're historians, but it struck a chord with us. We were smitten by the idea of preserving plants that had largely been forgotten."

The vintage vegetables and old-time ornamentals are only part of the historical connection. The garden layout—the shape of beds, the arrangement of flowers, the style of enclosures—also takes its cues from traditional gardening practices. "We found we could solve many a modern-day problem by studying historical

David (in red shirt) and
Paul take their vegetable
gardening seriously.

gardens," says Paul. When it came to providing some badly
needed privacy, for instance, he screened the garden from public
view with a dry stone wall, the type that has been a fixture of
English gardens for centuries. Without a drop of mortar, Paul
laid the masonry according to a prescribed pattern—two runs
of stone with rubble to fill the spaces and tie-stones to secure the
wall into position—to a height of about six feet (2 m). For some,
wall building can be the epitome of tedium, but for Paul it was
therapeutic, so satisfying that he eventually built several more
similar enclosures. "A relative of Paul, who was a construction
engineer, once estimated we have about 10,000 tons of stone in
these walls." All of it is granite salvaged from barn foundations in
the farm neighbourhood.

Not only do the stone walls provide privacy, they create
what Paul calls an "outdoor room," the perfect backdrop for
the perennials salvaged from his grandmother's garden. But
as Paul perfected his masonry skills, he and David expanded

their gardening repertoire. "Within the walls, we soon laid out a vegetable patch," David says. "We started with salad fixings and had such great success that we moved on to garlic and other late-season vegetables." Here, the stone walls proved more than an aesthetic asset. They absorb the heat from the sun, squeezing an extra week or two out of the growing season. Anything susceptible to frost, such as squash and other late-to-mature vegetables, are planted closest to the walls.

Within a few years, the salvaged perennials had outgrown the confines of the walled garden. "That got the wheels turning," says David, of yet another project he and Paul devised—the creation of a herbaceous border on the opposite side of the house. "We transplanted enough iris rhizomes to start a garden 120 feet long and 20 feet wide (37 m x 6 m)." Amid the irises is a dazzling array of poppies, phlox, day lilies, peonies and other transplanted perennials, all arranged according to some long-respected horticultural rules of thumb. For example, there is not a straight line to be seen, in keeping with the great English artist William Hogarth's decree that the eye should always follow a curve. "He suggested that an S-curve is the ultimate line of beauty," Paul states. Moreover, there is order to the arrangement of height, shape and colour in each bed, according to the recommendations of Gertrude Jekyll, the pre-eminent 19th-century English garden designer who suggested, among other things, that hot colours—reds, yellows, oranges—are shown to best effect in the centre, while cooler tones should be reserved for the ends.

Meanwhile, back in the walled garden, old roses have taken the place vacated by the transplanted perennials. In keeping with their historical themes, Paul and David have a preference for the traditional type that have stood the test of time. But in recent years, even these have taken a back seat to yet another phase in their gardening adventure, one that involves surprisingly few plants. "At the back of the house, sloping toward a man-made pond, we have built a Celtic garden," David explains. "Our friend, Beth Pierce Robinson, helped us enormously." To the uninitiated, it looks like a haphazard arrangement of pink-granite boulders, but is in fact rich in the lore of the ancients. According to Celtic ritual, the pond represents a haven safe from the wilderness, while the rocks along the path leading to it are symbolic of the journey toward sanctuary. Most important of all is a six-foot (2 m) "keystone." On the summer solstice, the sun rises directly above it. "A Celtic garden inspires not with plants but with

interesting shapes, drawing the eye toward focal points and vistas. It's very contemplative."

For David and Paul, contemplation is only one of the rewards of their gardening hobby. They have also taken pleasure in designing and planning their outdoor refuge and take great satisfaction in an afternoon of puttering. But most of all, gardening is all about self-expression. With history as their guide, Paul and David have lots to say.

1. Herbaceous border
2. Vegetable garden
3. Rose garden
4. Stone wall
5. Herb garden
6. Cedar hedge
7. Pasture
8. Rail fence
9. Celtic garden
10. Pond

Vintage Vegetables and Old-Time Ornamentals

IF YOU HAVE yet to be persuaded of the merits of heirloom vegetables, Paul says, "One taste of a Brandywine tomato is all the convincing you'll need." A variety long forgotten in the wake of the ever-popular Big Beef and Tiny Tim hybrids, the Brandywine has an unmistakably robust flavour, far more memorable than anything you'd buy at the grocery store. And it's the same with Paul's Boston Marrow squash, Connecticut Field pumpkins, Long Scarlet radishes and other produce: all are traditional varieties.

Using very little plant material, the Celtic garden is yet another theme modelled along historical lines.

As he says, "Heirlooms simply taste better."

The produce now considered "heirloom" was once standard fare in the family vegetable patch, but things changed when supermarkets got into the act. "No longer was taste the number one criterion for growing vegetables," David explains. "Supermarkets demanded lettuce that wouldn't wilt on store shelves, tomatoes that wouldn't bruise in transit and carrots that would all ripen at the same time. Before long, flavour was bred right out of them in favour of other traits." In the rush to conform, traditional varieties quickly fell from grace and today, some are quite rare indeed.

Paul and David may have been converted by taste, but heirloom vegetables also satisfy their environmental conscience. "We worry about monoculture and the lack of biodiversity in today's vegetable gene pool," says Paul. "What if some deadly disease or environmental disaster wipes out conventional market gardening?" Don't laugh—if it can happen with elm trees, it can happen with lettuce or tomatoes, too. By perpetuating heirloom vegetables, however, Paul, David and other enthusiasts help to preserve the gene pool for future generations. At some point, their venerable, hardy veggies may well come to the rescue.

IN THIS ERA of mass production and standardization, ornamental plants have endured much the same fate as vegetables. Certain traditional varieties have nearly been lost as nursery stock becomes more and more specialized. "A handful of varieties dominate the commercial market," says Paul. "Meanwhile, many of the old ones are in danger of dying out."

Roses are the perfect example. Throughout the 20th century, they were bred for larger and larger flowers, and more of them. "No longer would a single flower suffice," Paul suggests. "They had to bloom all season long." In the meantime, other desirable characteristics—fragrance, hardiness, resistance to disease—were inadvertently bred out. "Roses developed a nasty reputation for being prone to insects and unsuited to cooler climates like ours."

But not Grandma's heirloom roses. After generations in ancestral gardens, they have proven themselves to be hardy and disease resistant. And in their own way, the old roses are just as beautiful as their modern cousins. Moreover, they have come in handy for a new generation of gardeners. When the Central Experimental Farm, a government agency in Ottawa, wanted to breed roses that could withstand a Canadian winter, they turned to heirloom plants as a basis for the breeding stock. The result was the Explorer series, which can be grown with easy success in Winnipeg and other locales where no rose had grown before. "It shows just how valuable heirloom plants can be for research."

In a walled quadrant to the rear of the house, the garden started with perennials and later graduated to roses.

AMY JO EHMAN

Mail Order Manors

Catalogue homes from the T. Eaton Co. still dot the prairie landscape.

THERE WAS A time when prairie folks bought just about everything they needed from the Eaton's catalogue—from the kitchen sink to the entire house around which it was built. It seems a distant memory now, but from 1910 until the dirty 30s, the T. Eaton Co. and other catalogue companies offered a variety of mail-order homes, which arrived in kits from west coast lumber mills by railcar. Everything for house construction was included, right down to the doorknobs and the window latches.

During the boom years on the Prairies, where trees are naturally scarce, house-shopping by catalogue was one of the quickest and most affordable ways to get a lovely, sturdy new home. So it was, in the spring of 1923, that Gustave Mandin hitched up the horses and collected his house from the railway station in Duck Lake, Saskatchewan, between Saskatoon and Prince Albert. Mandin had settled on a nearby farm in 1893 at the age of 16, after emigrating from France with his parents. In 1923, he moved his family into town to be closer to their church and school. They needed a home, so he ordered No. 680, "the Eadgley," for $2,000 from the Eaton's catalogue.

"When I was a kid, I always knew our house was special because it was one of the larger homes in Duck Lake," says Mandin's grandson Louis Piche, who has restored the house to look almost the same as it did when his grandfather built it.

Donna and Louis Piche are proud to have restored a classic Eaton's "Eadgely"—here it is, as shown in the 1920 catalogue and in the flesh (opposite).

While many catalogue houses have been abandoned on empty farms, or modernized by a generation that doesn't appreciate their historic character, Louis and his wife Donna have turned back the clock on their Eaton's house, which they acquired a decade ago, after Louis' mother passed away.

The old house needed work. One of the first things to go was the moose head, shot by Louis' grandfather 50 years before, stuffed and hanging in the front porch. But more importantly, the Piches replaced the inefficient windows, ripped off the porch to restore the verandah, and painted the house the original colours—white with burgundy trim, which was matched with a chip of colour uncovered on an old storm window.

Fortunately, the interior required little work. The extensive woodwork in B.C. Douglas fir was unpainted and in good condition. Much of the antique furniture, which was also purchased from the catalogue, was still in the house. Only the wood floors, worn by 80-odd years of traffic, needed to be replaced.

Louis was inspired by watching renovation programs on television and by a trip to visit his daughter Nicole, who was studying in Owen Sound, Ontario. "Driving past the dairy farms and acreages, I saw all these beautiful old homes that had been restored and were so well looked after," he says. "When we got back here, I said that's what we're going to do. We're not going to throw this old house away."

He was also inspired by a surprise visit by Les Henry of Saskatoon. Les is a retired agricultural adviser who had visited many rural homes during his career and was compiling a book about catalogue houses on the Canadian Prairies. "He was really impressed with our house," recalls Louis. Indeed, a photo of the house, before the restoration was complete, is included in Les' book *Catalogue Houses: Eaton's and Others*. The book profiles mail-order houses across the west—some in better condition than others—along with original drawings and a history of the companies that sold them.

Catalogue homes were such a lucrative business that many organizations, such as the United Grain Growers Ltd. and the University of Saskatchewan, offered kits for houses, barns and one-room schools through the mail. At the time, the farm economy was booming—the price of wheat had skyrocketed before and during World War I. Settlers who came to Canada with almost nothing quickly found themselves flush with cash. "When they started out, they had a sod shack or some

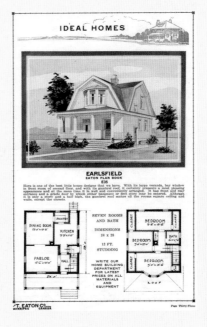

Within its distinctive barn roof, "the Earlsfield" was one of Eaton's most popular catalogue homes. Moved from its original location, this pristine example stands nicely maintained near Pike Lake, Saskatchewan.

sort of rudimentary house that could be built quickly. And now they had the money and wanted to build something that made a statement," explains Les.

In fact, he says, it was unscrupulous lumber companies ripping off the farmers that inspired Eaton's to include houses in its catalogue in the first place. "Eaton's advantage was that it was already established as a reliable business. You could send your money away in an envelope and something you wanted would come back," Les says.

There are hundreds of catalogue houses still standing across the Prairies but many people don't know they're living in a mail-order house. Others are buying empty catalogue houses off farmsteads and moving them into town, where the old walls once again become filled with the sounds and smells of domestic life. Still, few catalogue houses are as lovingly preserved as the Mandin-Piche home in Duck Lake. "All my cousins are happy that we're here, and the house has stayed in the family," says Piche. "I tell them I'm just keeping it until the next generation takes over."

Viva Verandahs!

by Tom Cruickshank

A VERANDAH IS THE best thing about buying an older home," exclaims Nancy Thomas. Her house was built over 100 years ago, when virtually every new dwelling was equipped with a spacious verandah. It's easy to understand her enthusiasm, for there is something undeniably inviting about a front porch. "It is a place to relax when work is done, to watch the world go by as the day winds down," she says. "Besides, the house would look naked without it."

Architects and other academics who study such things are more technical in their descriptions, but equally enamoured. In a lecture to students at the University of Toronto, sociologist A.T. Smith once said that verandahs and porches contribute enormously, if unwittingly, to street life and healthy neighbourhood relations, even in big cities. They create what he called "transitional space"—not public, but not entirely private either—that helps neighbours get to know each other as they watch daily comings and goings.

Hoop trim frames the view from within.

The verandah on Fred and
Nancy Thomas' home in
Port Hope, Ontario.

Trellis supports are a mark of a
pre-Confederation verandah.

"Verandahs allow contact with the outside world without having to leave the comfort of home," said Smith. "They are a 'safe' place where we can go about our own business while watching others go about theirs." He also said that today's builders are recognizing that modern, faceless architecture does little to encourage friendly social interaction. "Perhaps this explains why the verandah is making a comeback, even in large city housing projects."

Nancy and her husband, Fred, didn't need a lecture to be convinced of the merits of their front porch. "It was one of the selling points of this house," Fred recalls of their first sight of the house back in 1978. "The verandah curves around the south and east sides of the building. It's integral to the architecture, and we knew we would be using it every chance we could."

Back in the early 19th century, the verandah was a novel idea. Adorned with curlicue trim, it amounted to a roofed deck, about six feet (2 m) wide, and often wrapped around three, if not all four, sides of the house. The English borrowed the concept from India, and it made its first appearance in Canada in the 1830s. The verandah was the first architectural amenity to acknowledge the great outdoors, offering the opportunity to "take exercise" after a meal or relax on a rocking chair. Never before was an open-air "room" so integral to house design; never before had something so fanciful become part of the Canadian architectural tradition.

The verandah had an undeniably romantic appeal, but it also had a practical side. Like a giant awning, it shaded the house from the worst heat of summer, helping to keep the indoor temperature cool. In a clever twist, the verandah did the opposite in winter, allowing the sun, so low in the sky, to penetrate the house when its heat was needed most.

The most alluring of early verandahs were supported by wooden trellises, not posts. These are rare today, owing not only to the whims of fashion but fussy maintenance. More familiar are chamfered posts or turned posts, which made their appearance in the 1860s. By then, gingerbread trim was routinely strung along the verandah cornice, with wonderfully whimsical results.

Unlike some novelties, the verandah never fell from fashion. It was popular throughout the 19th century and, in different styles, persevered into the 20th. It is still with us—no house in the country is complete without one.

In verandah-speak, the concave rafters are officially called a "bowed roof."

An arcaded effect is nothing if not charming.

ABOVE Pure Victorian whimsy

LEFT Spoolwork and turret turn an ordinary farmhouse into a striking architectural exercise.

Care and Maintenance

THE VERANDAH IS undeniably beautiful, but it is actually quite fragile. There is little to protect it from the elements, and, since it is close to the ground, it is an easy target for insects. But you can extend the life of a verandah if you keep watch for signs of trouble.

• Verandahs and porches are constructed entirely of wood. You can prolong the life of the wood with regular painting and repair. Fill small cracks before they grow large. Replace rotted sections with fresh lumber. Keep steps, decks and other close-to-the-ground components elevated from contact with the soil. Be sure no opportunities exist for water to pool. All components should drain (i.e., handrails should be tilted slightly to shed water; floors need not be absolutely horizontal).

• Once a year, take a close look at the roof for signs of moisture damage. Are the shingles and flashing sound? Check the condition of gutters and downspouts.

• Examine paint for peeling, cracking or blisters. Correct the source of the problem before repainting.

• Decaying steps are not only a safety hazard, but because they touch the ground, they often show the first signs of moisture and/or insect damage. Scrutinize their condition carefully.

• Is the deck still in good shape? Does it slope away from the house? Check the floorboards for warped planks and protruding nails.

• Check the posts, especially the base, for rot.

• Examine the joint between the wall of the house and the verandah roof. If you see any gaps, it's a sure sign that moisture is seeping into the woodwork.

• Check the latticework and foundation closely. If the house has settled over the years, these may be touching the ground.

• Don't seal the crawl space under the floor. It is important that it remains adequately vented to inhibit moisture. That's why latticework has been used traditionally—it keeps skunks at bay and still provides plenty of air circulation.

MARC HUMINILOWYCZ

Catch a Falling Star

Every August, watch the best show in the sky

IT'S ALWAYS FUN to marvel at the amazing spectacle of stars on a clear night in the country. But there's one celestial event that stands out as a real treat for stargazers. It's the Perseid meteor shower, which occurs every summer. If nothing else, it reminds us that we're just another speck floating in space, and that there's a lot happening beyond our atmosphere.

We've all seen them before—those momentary flashes of light streaking across the night sky. Commonly referred to as "shooting stars" they are, in fact, meteors. They begin as tiny fragments of space debris emanating from comets racing toward the sun. As small as a grain of sand, this debris burns up when it hits our atmosphere, causing brief but brilliant flashes of blue-green light.

Meteors are visible on a clear night at any time of year, with the highest number, maybe three or four per hour, occurring from about 1:00 a.m. until dawn. But at certain times, as the earth orbits around the sun and its dark side passes through large amounts of comet debris, the night sky puts on an incredible show.

The Perseid meteor shower, so called because of its location in the Perseus constellation in the northeastern sky, happens around mid-August. Perseids are burning fragments of the comet Swift-Tuttle, which has been gradually disintegrating for thousands of years on its many journeys around the sun. They're fast meteors, lasting only a few seconds, and they tend to be fairly bright on average. If you're lucky, you might see a spectacular fireball, as larger comet fragments burn into oblivion. So put on a pot of coffee and get ready to stay up late (or get up really early) for the best show on the planet. You can always catch up on your sleep the next day.

Prepping for the Perseids

· Set yourself up in the darkest zone in your neck of the woods.

· Facing the northeast sky, lie on a blanket on the ground, set up a reclining lawn chair or lie on the hood of your car leaning against the windshield.

· Leave the binoculars inside. You get a better view with the naked eye.

· Is it a star or a planet? The answer is easy—stars twinkle, planets don't.

· As you gaze at the Big Dipper, remember that its stars are about 70 light years away from us, meaning that what you're seeing has taken a human lifetime to travel through space to reach your eye.

DAN NEEDLES

The Slow Food Chain

True confessions from the Ninth Concession

THIS PLOT OF GROUND should be hugely productive. Every year, I fatten lambs, pigs and a steer for the freezer. The orchard produces apples, pears and plums. I keep a flock of laying hens and a large garden. But there always seems to be some hiccup between the barn and the kitchen table.

I milked a cow and two goats for several years until the kids eventually turned their noses up at it in favour of the store-bought variety. Our free-range chickens were so tough they had to be simmered for several hours before you could eat them. My wife doesn't eat lamb and my daughter has become a vegetarian. A single spray of the orchard now costs $17, which would buy enough apples at the local market to last us all winter.

My wife long ago returned to the supermarket to ensure a stable food supply in our house and, about a year ago, she began buying the new Omega-3 milk and eggs. Some television host convinced her that we need extra linoleic acid in our diet to reduce the incidence of heart attack and stroke. I was a skeptic until I attended the Farmsmart Conference at the University of Guelph last winter where an eminent professor said exactly the same thing and tipped me off that I could produce my very own Omega-3 eggs, just by feeding flaxseed to my hens.

On the way home, I picked up a bag of flax at the feed store and added it at the rate of one big scoop to a 50-pound bag of lay mash. Then I sat back and waited for the health benefits to roll in. Of course, the effects aren't immediate. It takes about 90 days for the stuff to work its way through to the eggs, which is a long time in the life of a chicken around here. Then, just as the eggs were reaching their maximum Omega-3 potency, a family of skunks burrowed under the henhouse and started swiping the eggs. I plugged that hole and some raccoons quickly made another one, ate several hens and traumatized the flock so badly that they stopped laying altogether. So the eggs didn't actually make it to the table. But we did notice a statistically significant reduction in the incidence of stroke and heart attack in the local raccoon and skunk populations. They appear to be healthier than ever.

This is often the way it goes out here. I have lost count of those failed enterprises that began with some "Aha!" moment late at night in bed while I leafed through some obscure poultry magazine. "I wish you'd read *Penthouse* like other husbands," says my wife.

I now have three breeds of chickens. I bought Araucanas first because they lay those blue-shelled eggs that are supposed to be cholesterol-free, if you believe the promotional literature that comes with them. Next, I invested in Chanteclers because they have very small combs that are supposed to be less susceptible to freezing than other chickens. Finally I found Cornish game hens that are dual-purpose and will actually set and hatch the eggs of the other two breeds.

> "I wish you'd read *Penthouse* like other husbands," says my wife.

None of this is working the way I planned. Although the Chanteclers do lay an egg now and then, their rooster froze his comb last winter and has been shooting blanks ever since. The Araucana rooster drowned himself in the horse trough after Dougie, the visiting pot-bellied pig, performed certain unspeakable acts on him late one night. The Cornish rooster is intact and enthusiastic but his mate is not laying any eggs at all after that raccoon incident. She has been sulking silently on a dish of cat kibble for over three months now.

My wife says you know there is a problem in the laying flock when you hear yourself saying that you're going out to the henhouse "to get the egg."

The professor insists that health benefits delivered directly in our food—or "nutraceuticals" as they are called—are the exciting new wave of the future in food production. For the moment, however, we will have to make do with a spoonful of cod liver oil at breakfast.

A Taste of Summer

by Darlene King

Sesame Roasted Broccoli & Green Beans

ROASTING THE vegetable in this recipe brings out the very best flavours. This side dish is a welcome accompaniment to grilled beef.

SERVES 6 TO 8

1 lb	green beans, trimmed	454 g
1 lb	broccoli, cut lengthwise into quarters, then in half	454 g
2 Tbsp	oyster sauce	30 ml
2 Tbsp	medium-dry sherry	30 ml
1 Tbsp	canola oil	15 ml
1 tsp	sesame oil	5 ml
2 Tbsp	white sesame seeds	30 ml

Preheat the oven to 400°F (200°C).

Lightly oil a roasting pan. Place the green beans and broccoli in the pan.

Mix the oyster sauce, sherry, canola oil and sesame oil in a small bowl. Pour the mixture over the green beans and broccoli. Lightly toss the vegetables and the mixture together so that the vegetables are evenly coated. Place in the oven and bake for 10 minutes.

Remove from the oven and turn the vegetables. Evenly sprinkle the sesame seeds over the vegetables. Return roasting pan to the oven and bake for 5 minutes longer.

Tomato Bruschetta, Three Ways

MAKES 24 APPETIZERS

12	mini pita pockets	12

ORANGE TOMATO RECIPE

3	medium orange tomatoes, diced	3
3 Tbsp	extra-virgin olive oil	45 ml
2 Tbsp	chopped coriander	30 ml
1	clove garlic, finely chopped	1
½ tsp	cumin seed	2.5 ml

Stir all ingredients in a medium-sized bowl and set aside. Refrigerate until ready to serve.

RED TOMATO RECIPE

3	medium red tomatoes, diced	3
3 Tbsp	extra-virgin olive oil	45 ml
2 Tbsp	chopped basil	30 ml
1	clove garlic, finely chopped	1

Stir all ingredients in a medium-sized bowl. Refrigerate until ready to serve.

YELLOW TOMATO RECIPE

3	medium yellow tomatoes, diced	3
¼ cup	black olives, pitted and chopped	60 ml
3 Tbsp	extra-virgin olive oil	45 ml
2 Tbsp	fresh parsley	30 ml
1	clove garlic, finely chopped	1
½ tsp	freshly grated lemon zest	2.5 ml

Stir all ingredients in a medium-sized bowl and set aside. Refrigerate until ready to serve.

UNHEARD OF in mainstream kitchens even a decade ago, bruschetta has become a mainstay on restaurant menus and among hobby chefs. Our bruschetta is actually three different variations on the theme, each with its unique flavour and colour.

Preheat the oven to 375°F (190°C).

Slice each pita pocket in half, on the horizontal. Lightly brush with olive oil. Place on a baking sheet and bake for 10 minutes or until crispy. Remove from oven to cool. (If pitas are not available, thinly sliced baguette is certainly acceptable.)

To serve, spoon a little of the tomato mixture onto the pita.

Pancetta, Pecan and Sun-dried Tomato Pasta

SERVES 4

6 cups	cooked penne pasta	1.5 l
¼ cup	olive oil	60 ml
2	large garlic cloves, finely chopped	2
¼ lb	pancetta or bacon, diced	113 g
¾ cup	pecan, lightly chopped	170 ml
½ cup	oil-packed sun-dried tomatoes, drained and lightly chopped	120 ml
2 cups	cherry tomatoes, sliced in half	480 ml
¼ cup	fresh basil, chopped	60 ml
½ cup	grated Parmesan cheese	120 ml

SUMMERTIME IS synonymous with fresh tomatoes and herbs, so here's a pasta dish full of Italian gusto just perfect for the season.

Prepare pasta according to package directions. Drain and place in a large bowl. Toss with 2 Tbsp of olive oil.

Heat the remaining olive oil in a sauté pan over medium heat. Add pancetta and cook until lightly browned. Add garlic and cook for 30 seconds longer. Using a slotted spoon, remove the pancetta and garlic and add it to the pasta. Leave the oil in the pan.

Return pan to the heat and sauté the pecans until lightly toasted. Using a slotted spoon, remove the pecans and add to the pasta. Add the sun-dried tomatoes to the pan and sauté for 1 minute. Add the cherry tomatoes to the pan and heat them through slightly. Add the tomatoes to the pasta along with any drippings left in the pan.

Stir the chopped basil and Parmesan cheese into the pasta. Toss well. Garnish with a few shavings of Parmesan cheese and serve.

Oriental Chicken Kebabs

with Pineapple and Mango

SERVES 6

1 cup	soya sauce	240 ml
½ cup	honey	120 ml
¼ cup	vegetable oil	60 ml
¼ cup	sesame oil	60 ml
¼ cup	hoisin sauce	60 ml
¼ cup	molasses	60 ml
¼ cup	brown sugar	60 ml
¼ cup	medium dry sherry	60 ml
4 tsp	garlic, chopped	20 ml
2 tsp	fresh ginger, minced	10 ml
	freshly grated black pepper	
4	boneless chicken breasts, cut into 2-inch (5 cm) cubes	4
1	mango, peeled and cubed	1
1	pineapple, peeled and cubed	1
6	skewers	6
2 Tbsp	sesame seeds	30 ml

KEBABS ARE fast and easy to make. Serve over rice along with asparagus bundles for a meal that's elegant to look at and tasty, too. Best of all, all the prep work is done before your guests arrive.

In a medium bowl, combine soya sauce, honey, vegetable oil, sesame oil, hoisin sauce, molasses, brown sugar, sherry, garlic, ginger and black pepper and mix well. Add chicken pieces and marinate in the refrigerator for 2 hours.

Remove chicken from marinade. Bring marinade to a boil and simmer for 10 minutes or longer, until it begins to thicken. Remove from heat.

Place a small amount in a bowl to be used as a baste for the chicken during cooking. The remainder can be served warm as a sauce for the kebabs.

Preheat grill to medium-high heat. Thread chicken pieces onto wooden or metal skewers, alternating meat with mango and pineapple pieces. Reduce heat to medium.

Place kebabs on slightly oiled grill. Close lid and continue to cook for approximately 10 minutes direct grilling, turning and basting occasionally with reserved marinade. Chicken is ready when no longer pink on the inside.

Remove from heat and sprinkle with sesame seeds.

Serve with reserved sauce.

(Option: Asparagus Bundles: Make asparagus bundles by tying 2 or 3 spears together with butcher's twine. Parboil bundles in salted water for 3 to 4 minutes. Drain and run under cold water. Refrigerate.

A few minutes before the chicken is cooked, place the bundles on the grill to reheat. Baste with a little melted butter.)

autumn

autumn comforts

I F YOU'RE OF a certain age, you remember the energy crisis of the 1970s when, for political reasons, the price of oil skyrocketed into the stratosphere. Come the heating season that first autumn, homeowners watched their savings literally go up the chimney flue, and they quickly realized that their houses squandered alarming amounts of precious energy. Ever since, they've been looking for ways to improve things, at first to save money and later, as part of an effort to tread lightly upon the earth.

It was about this time that *Harrowsmith* first appeared, eager to show readers that there were alternatives to oil heat and the other trappings of conventional dwellings. The magazine was one of the first to embrace wood as a cheaper and more sustainable heating option and, unlike other magazines that revelled in paint colours and decorator fabrics, *Harrowsmith* was more interested in presenting homes that embraced the conserver ethic.

At first, many of the houses we profiled were decidedly homespun efforts such as passive-solar geodesic domes and log cabins with no link to the outside world. Nowadays, in step with the times, homeowners seem less willing to sacrifice creature comforts, but we still think there's more to building a house than impressing the neighbours. Indeed, sustainable architecture can be as inviting as it is efficient, and come fall, when the thermostat is reset after a long hot summer, therein lies the real beauty of a *Harrowsmith* home.

A homestead seems to come into its own in the autumn. As the days grow shorter and cooler, our focus turns indoors, and we appreciate home comforts and improvements all the more. It is also in autumn that rural dwellers are thankful for some of the best rituals of the year. With the scent of wood smoke in the air, this is the time to savour the last tomato and the first apple, not to mention the bounty of squash, leeks and other cool-weather vegetables fresh from the garden. But of all the traditions specific to the season, the one that is perhaps the most anticipated is the visit to the annual fall fair. Although the conventional rural fair faces competition from any manner of new, themed festivals and celebrations, it is still the social glue that holds many a rural community together.

For most country people, the fair offers a chance to see neighbours and friends after the long harvest, but you should never forget that the event is more than fun and games. For serious farmers, there is much prestige at stake in the livestock shows and for anyone keen on improving bloodlines or other agricultural advances, the fair is a great place to acquire the latest information. And, as more non-farm people flock to the countryside, county fairs are adapting to the times. Today, rare is the fair that doesn't offer something of specific interest to rural homeowners. And as energy efficiency and sustainable architecture emerge as being more and more important to the mainstream, you can bet you can find some booths devoted to such topics as wood heat, passive solar and straw bale houses. For *Harrowsmith Country Life* readers, there's something poetic here, isn't there?

A Straw Bale Homestead

by Tom Cruickshank

WITH SMILES ACROSS their faces, John Wise and Anita Jansman call their farm "Wise Acres." A firm believer in the organic ethic, John has been a farmer for 25 years and runs what used to be called a "mixed operation"—a little of this, a little of that on 100 acres in the heart of Lennox and Addington County in eastern Ontario. Over the seasons, he has raised chickens and beef cattle, grown his share of vegetables, established a pick-your-own berry patch and tried his luck with various organic grains, including fall wheat, corn and barley. "I've grown it all," John muses, "but never in my wildest dreams did I imagine that someday I would grow my own house."

Like an old-fashioned barn-raising, family and friends pitch in to help pack the wooden house frame with straw bales.

But that's exactly what he did in the summer of 2000, as he and Anita made plans to build a new straw bale home on their property. "Unlike some people who choose straw bale construction, I was in the position of being able to grow my own building materials," John continues. "Not many homeowners can say that." He lost count, but reckons his plans called for something less than 500 bales of straw, left over from his wheat crop, which he gathered from a 10-acre field.

Straw has been used in home construction since the days of the three little pigs. Traditionally, it was stuffed by the pitchforkful into walls to plug drafts and, of course, it made a dandy thatched roof. But it wasn't until after the invention of the baling machine in the 1870s, that some savvy builder figured a nice tight cube of straw could be used as the basis for an entire house. Faced with a shortage of wood, prairie homesteaders in Nebraska were the first to use baled straw as building blocks. It mattered not a whit that the houses were primitive in the extreme: They were surprisingly cozy against the elements, not to mention durable. Indeed, some of those early straw bale houses are still standing today.

Bale construction faded from the map for subsequent generations until the energy crisis reared its ugly head in the 1970s. In the scramble to find energy-conserving building materials, the amazing efficiency of straw bale couldn't be overlooked. "Although technologically simple, straw bales are one of the best insulators known to man," explains John. "A straw wall—one bale thick—has an insulating value of R40, which is hard to duplicate with fibreglass batts or other conventional materials." Moreover, there are no gaps, which creates an unbroken insulating surface. In contrast, a standard wall can never be as efficient, since only the cavity between the studs, not the studs themselves, are insulated.

Straw bale has another ace up its environmental sleeve: It is as close as the nearest farmer's field. Enough straw is already produced every year in North America to meet all our residential building requirements. Not only would this make use of a material that would otherwise go to waste (farmers haven't got much use for straw other than as mulch or bedding for livestock), but also straw houses require fewer conventional materials—bricks, stone, concrete, mortar, lumber—thus lightening the demand on finite resources, not to mention the energy used shipping them around the country. John remarks, "If ever there was a material

All their planning and hard work has paid off—Anita and John pose in front of their eco-conscious, energy-efficient home.

tailor-made for the environmentally conscious, it has to be bale."

If John and Anita had had to buy their own, the bales would have cost them a paltry $750. "That's not a lot to pay for four walls, but don't assume that a straw bale house is inherently cheap," John explains.

John figures their project set them back perhaps more than a conventional dwelling of similar size and style. "But let's compare apples to apples. It would've cost the earth to get R40 performance in standard walls, and even then, I doubt we'd have the same level of comfort." During their first winter in the house, John boasts, he and Anita never once felt a draft. "Nor can you discount the energy savings, which will go a long way in helping this house to pay for itself." The couple's primary source of heat is a wood stove, which in some winters burns a mere two cords of wood. Also at the ready is a propane-fired radiant floor heating system—an ingenious network of hot-fluid tubes embedded in the concrete floor, which dispense auxiliary heat throughout the house. Although expensive to install, the radiant heat requires little propane throughout the year. No wonder John says that, weighing the costs, straw bale is superb value.

While straw is the conversation piece that makes bale construction so unique, it is actually only part of the story. Every straw bale house is coated, inside and out, in a sheath of lime plaster stucco. It is applied over a wire mesh attached to the straw. Engineers call it a "stress skin panel" for its significant structural capacity, but it is also the waterproof seal that protects the straw from the ravages of the elements. Aesthetically, it can be rendered smooth, but a rough, rustic finish, often dyed in earth tones, gets the nod from most straw builders.

For all its noble attributes, bale is still largely unproven, at least in the minds of the mainstream. Although gaining in popularity—there were only five straw houses in Ontario in 1997; at last count, there are now over 100—it is rare that the technique is recognized by local building codes. "That proved to be an obstacle," admits John, saying that municipal clerks stood scratching their heads when he presented his plans to them. "Unlike a conventional house, our plans required an architect's and an engineer's stamp before the local building department would approve them." However, times are changing and word is getting around. In 1995, the U.S. Department of Energy recognized the thermal capabilities of straw bale as a construction material; meanwhile, straw has been written into the building codes of California, Colorado and a few other states. Closer to home, the star attraction at the 2001 Fall Home Show at Exhibition Place in Toronto was none other than a straw bale house.

NATURALISTS AT HEART, John and Anita first heard about bale construction through the environmental grapevine and followed up with a search on the Internet. Little did they know they'd find a builder so close at hand. Less than an hour away in Madoc, Ontario, business partners Chris Magwood and Peter Mack had plenty of experience with the technique, with 32 straw houses behind them and a fervent enthusiasm for their craft. "We hired them for the technical stuff," says Anita. "But it was up to us to come up with a layout."

Characterized by a deliberately uneven stucco finish, straw adapts well to the rustic, homemade look and lends itself to funky, unconventional designs. "We liked its down-home appeal,"

Generous windows flood the two-storey living area with light.

says Anita, "and we especially liked its structural versatility: There were few constraints as we drew up our dream home." In consultation with Toronto architect Janet Stewart, the couple kept four crucial criteria in mind to guide their design:

• An open-concept living area, unencumbered by partition walls. Living space, dining room and kitchen are, in effect, one large room under a two-storey cathedral ceiling. At the peak, the ceiling reaches 24 feet (7.3 m), providing ample headroom for a master suite loft. Bonus: the open arrangement, with opposing windows on all four walls, does wonders for cross-ventilation. In winter, a ceiling fan compensates for the high ceiling, helping to distribute heat more evenly.

• A tower, a fun indulgence much like an old-fashioned widow's walk. Here, John can play amateur astronomer and preside over his fields. Bonus: with the windows open on a hot summer night, the tower sucks up stale air from the living area and dispenses it outside. "We have no need for air conditioning," John boasts.

• A screened porch about 11 feet by 15 feet (3.4 m by 4.5 m), larger and more functional than a traditional verandah, where, as John suggests, "we can hear the crickets without being eaten alive."

• A basement suite, complete with a bathroom and two bedrooms. Hardly a primitive root cellar, the fully finished basement is the domain of Anita's two teenage sons. "When they fly the coop in a few years," she says, "it will function as room for guests."

The open concept follows a logical sequence of space allocation. Dining area and kitchen are sequestered under the second-storey loft bedroom, while the living area takes full advantage of the cathedral ceiling. The view from the upstairs loft provides a unique outlook over the living area.

Janet honed their back-of-an-envelope ideas into an engaging and highly personal plan that, with its lofty tower, looks like it is modelled after a country church. Because the walls were so high—three storeys including the tower, making it the tallest straw structure in Canada—it was decided that bales alone wouldn't provide enough structural strength, so an auxiliary post-and-beam frame was employed to take up the slack. Normally, for the load-bearing type of straw bale, the entire weight of the building is borne by the bales and the stucco walls. To ensure that the bales settle consistently, they are secured together with wire or cable ties. Load-bearing bale houses can be remarkably inexpensive.

Having chosen a site 600 feet (183 m) from the road— "as far away from traffic as possible"—the next step in the construction was digging a hole. "The foundation is thoroughly ordinary," John confesses. "The fun didn't start until Chris, Peter and the rest of the crew arrived."

Camping out in tents beside the construction site, the straw bale team set to work. The first thing they did was to lay a "bale curb"—two parallel lines of 2 x 4s—around the perimeter of the floor. "This is the base on which the first bales rest, giving them clearance as an extra precaution against the unlikely event of a flood," John explains. Next, up went the wood framing and the skeletal roof, and before long came the moment everyone was waiting for: "Bale Day."

Bale Day is like an old-fashioned barn-raising bee, in which not only the hired crew, but the clients, family, friends and neighbours gather to stuff the frame full of straw. "It's a real hands-on experience, almost a party," Anita says, recalling how quickly the walls went up. "The whole house was stuffed to the rafters in less than a day." Toting and lifting the 35-pound (16 kg) bales and heaving them into place, each volunteer was responsible for his own section of the walls, staggering each bale as if building a brick wall. Gaps were packed with loose straw, completely engulfing the wooden frame. The fit is snug, but not so tight that the bales compress—compacted straw loses its insulation capacity. "We had ladders and movable scaffolding on hand to make the upper reaches accessible—and it's a good thing we had my hay elevator handy for the tower," John adds. "Things got messy really quickly. Stray straw was everywhere. If we misplaced something—say, a hammer or sunglasses—it was buried for the duration."

Even with the bales in place, the work had barely begun. From this point, Chris and Peter's crew took over, preparing the walls for the finishing touch: the stucco skins. As John explains, "This requires a wire mesh, that is, a surface that will accept the stucco." First, the crew sewed the mesh to the straw with giant needles and baling wire. In all, four applications were required: a rough coat inside and out applied with a gun, and then a finer, colour-dyed coat, also inside and out, applied by trowel.

With the roof on and the walls enclosed, the exotic chapters of John and Anita's story soon came to a close. "From then on, ours was much like any other house-building project," muses John. There was plumbing to install, a kitchen to design, and decisions over everything from paint colours to faucet styles. But when it was all done, the results were anything but ordinary. "It isn't everyone who can say they grew their own house," John says. It brings new meaning to the term, "home grown."

Bale Infill and Hybrid Straw Construction

In addition to the load-bearing type of straw bale construction, there are the "bale infill" and the "hybrid." Bale infill incorporates a wood-frame skeleton as the structural component, with bale filling in the spans between timbers. Straw takes none of the load, acts only as insulation and is covered in clapboard or some other conventional siding. The hybrid also incorporates a wood frame, but bales also bear some of the load and the rough-cast stucco walls remain the dominant visual component. Hybrids allow for greater flexibility of design, although the price is substantially higher. When assessing John and Anita's blueprints, a frame was deemed necessary in light of the height of the walls and the span of the open concept plan.

A Lesson in Straw Structure

IF YOU'VE never lived in farm country, you might think a bale is a bale is a bale. Not so, when it comes to home construction. Only straw bales, not hay bales, are suitable for building. Straw is the dead residue left over from a grain crop. Already dry, its hollow structure and inherent strength make it an ideal building material. Hay is something else altogether: field grasses cut while still green and baled for use as livestock feed. High in moisture content and rich in nutrients, hay would certainly rot if used in house construction.

And of course, the big round bales so popular today won't work with bale construction. Only square bales will do, and although size doesn't really matter, the bales should be consistent. Remember, certain measurements, such as the height of window sills and the walls themselves, are to some degree dependent on the modular heights of the bales.

Although straw makes bale construction so unique, it is only part of the story. Every straw bale house is coated, inside and out, in a sheath of lime plaster stucco. It is applied over a wire mesh attached to the straw. Engineers call it a "stress skin panel" for its significant structural capacity, but it is also the waterproof seal that protects the straw from the ravages of the elements. Aesthetically, it can be rendered smooth, but a rough, rustic finish, often dyed in earth tones, gets the nod from most straw builders.

1 To insure against rain damage, bale enthusiasts recommend that the roof be in place before the bales are installed. However, the roofing material didn't arrive on schedule, so the crew took their chances and prayed for a sunny day. Meanwhile, the tower was assembled on site and later hoisted into place.

2 John arrives with the first load of bales.

3 Dimensions of the house are based largely on the modular size of a single bale.

4 Like some kind of monumental sewing project, Chris (on the outside) secures the mesh to the straw with a giant needle and thread. Peter waits on the inside to feed it back.

5 Wire mesh extends to the ground, over the exposed sections of the frame and foundation, ready to receive the first coat of stucco.

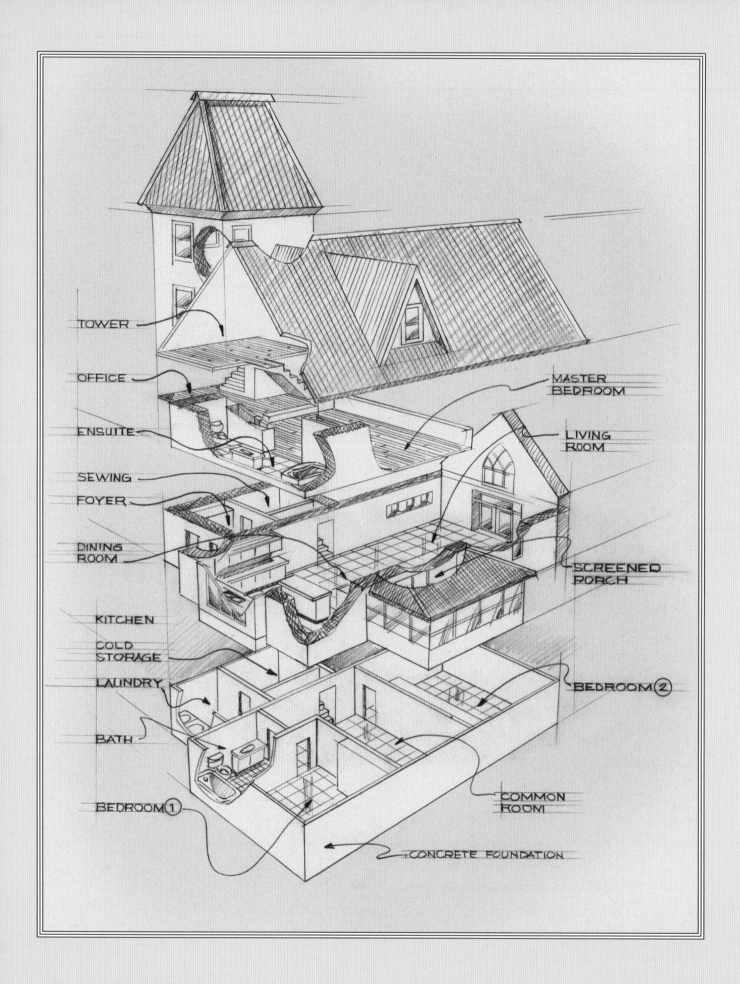

TOWER

OFFICE

ENSUITE

SEWING

FOYER

DINING
ROOM

KITCHEN

COLD
STORAGE

LAUNDRY

BATH

BEDROOM ①

MASTER
BEDROOM

LIVING
ROOM

SCREENED
PORCH

BEDROOM ②

COMMON
ROOM

CONCRETE FOUNDATION

Specs

CONCEPT: Straw bale construction on post and beam frame; open-plan design. Owner acted as general contractor. Straw bale contractors: Chris Magwood and Peter Mack, Madoc, Ontario. Architect: Janet Stewart, Toronto.

GENESIS: Built summer 2000, occupied fall 2000.

LOCATION: Centreville, Ontario, north of Napanee.

BEDROOMS: 3

BATHROOMS: 2

TOTAL USABLE FLOOR AREA: About 1,500 square feet (140 m²), including basement.

FOUNDATION: Conventional poured concrete.

STRUCTURE: Hybrid straw bale construction, bolstered by post and beam frame. Bales measure 18" x 36" (14" deep), laid on edge (bales settle more if laid like conventional bricks).

ROOF: Galvanized sheetmetal.

HEAT: Primary source: Wood stove; Supplemental source: in-floor radiant heating system, Rural Water, Tamworth, Ontario.

INSULATION: Walls: straw bales to R40 specifications; Ceiling: lightweight Roxul batts (Bales, of course, are too heavy for roof insulation).

ELECTRICAL SERVICE: 100 amp, Goulah Electric, Enterprise, Ontario. Note: house was wired with electrical boxes in place before baling.

WINDOWS: Double-glazed wood-frame units, including specialty Gothic picture windows.

FLOORS: Poured concrete (as integral part of the radiant heating system), Sousa Ready Mix, Kingston.

Beauty and the Beasts

by Dan Needles

IT'S FAIR DAY, and you've brought the kids down to ride the midway and listen to the bands play. If you're like most people, you might lean against the white board fence for a few minutes to watch smartly dressed men and women lead cows around a show ring. Next door, there's another group kneeling in the grass beside impossibly white, fluffy sheep, staring intently at a man in a suit with a fedora and a clipboard. You won't be the first person to ask, What is the point of all this?

For most of the participants, competing at the purebred livestock shows held across Canada in the fall is just a fun hobby. Love of fine animals and the camaraderie of the show circuit bring them back year after year. But at the top of the heap, there are real cash rewards, not necessarily in prize money, but in the increased market value that a championship ribbon from a prestigious show can bestow on an animal.

A livestock show is mostly good fun, but there are big dollars at stake for those who reach the top.

Even if the purse isn't much, a prize at a livestock show adds considerable value to sheep, cattle, horses and other barnyard animals.

It's expensive and time-consuming. There are entry fees, transport costs, accommodation and food for you and the animals, insurance, fitting supplies (items used to prepare an animal for show) and, of course, most of your spare time goes up in smoke. But purebred animals that win at the top horse and cattle shows find a ready market among the thousands of livestock producers across the country and south of the border who never enter the show ring themselves, but want to improve their own bloodlines. A champion beef bull at Regina's Agribition, the largest beef show in Canada, steps into a lucrative career as a national supplier of semen. A winning Holstein dairy cow at the Royal Winter Fair in Toronto adds thousands of dollars to her value overnight, and international buyers, who have great respect for Canadian dairy genetics, snap up her daughters.

What makes one animal superior to another? To the casual observer, Beaconglow's Laurabelle Lulu looks a lot like Mulmur

Meadows' Empress Divine. But to the trained eye, small differences in physical proportion say a great deal to the beef industry about what should be a priority in a cow. And when a respected judge at a premier event, like the Denver Beef Show, slaps the rump of a Black Angus bull and names him champion, the image of that animal burns into the retinas of Angus breeders across North America.

Not every livestock producer believes that judges should have this kind of power over the industry. Critics say it's all very subjective and has a history of leading breeders in the wrong direction on many occasions. For example, the founding fathers of the Royal in 1922 were mostly cattlemen and owners of fine Shorthorns, the most popular breed in Canada at the time. They were taken aback when the upstart Black Angus breed started winning all the ribbons because they were more compact than the Shorthorns. The judges said that the consumer wanted a smaller cut of beef and encouraged a whole generation of breeders to downsize their animals for the show ring. Cattlemen blindly followed the trend until the three Canadian breeds—Shorthorns, Herefords and Angus—all looked like shoe boxes on four feet.

Suddenly, in the 1950s, the trend reversed itself as judges decided that the consumer wanted bigger cuts of beef again. The poor Shorthorn didn't respond to the upsizing efforts and was quickly abandoned by the industry. Herefords and Angus didn't

Most farmers who exhibit their livestock at fairs aren't in it for the money.

Judges assess not only the physical appearance of an animal but also check how well it stands and how it moves.

fare any better. A few enterprising cattlemen began looking offshore to France, Britain and Australia for new breeds of cattle, and by the 1970s, the purebred industry had split into no less than two dozen different breed associations.

Canada's beef industry still hasn't fully recovered from the effects of that wild goose chase a half-century ago. And there are still lots of skeptics among rank-and-file cattlemen who question the whole spectacle. If you talk to the grizzled beef farmer sitting in the beer garden outside the show ring, he will probably dismiss every single one of the 30 active beef breeds listed by the Canadian Livestock Records in Ottawa. "Pampered, precious and pointless," he'll say, and go on to tell you how a good, honest, crossbred cow will perform better in the rugged conditions of the real world. But chances are also pretty good that the same man owns a purebred bull and paid a lot of money for it. This is one of the funny contradictions that helps to explain why the livestock shows still occupy an important place in the farm calendar.

JUDGES HAD A bit more success with dairy cows. Controversy erupted back in the 1920s when some exhibitors complained that ranking a cow on physical terms alone, without considering her ability to produce milk, reduced the whole exercise to a beauty contest. For the next 40 years, the debate raged until the then federal minister of agriculture, Harry Hayes, introduced a nationwide classification system that decreased the number of classes (groups of animals that are judged together), put a limit on entries and set production requirements. The Hayes system is still in place today. A cow can't get into the leading shows unless she has met stiff production goals. Once in the ring, she is judged on her physical strength and conformation (the manner in which an animal is formed). Does she stand on good strong legs? Is the udder well attached? Does she have the capacity to process the large amounts of feed she has to eat to be a top producer? The judge is looking at characteristics that encourage the production of milk, but no milk will flow if the cow's legs give out or her back can't support the weight of an enormous udder.

The beauty versus production debate had more than an academic significance for dairy farmers. By the 1960s, foreign buyers were raving about our stock, and the export market for Canadian dairy genetics was born. Today, our Holsteins are the top producers in herds around the world. But again, the skeptic points out that using the same 12 sires for so many years now has the Holstein swimming in the shallow end of the gene pool. The modern Holstein is plagued with reproductive problems that have drastically shortened her working life. Cows that used to produce for 15 years are now lucky to last 5.

HMMM... WELL, A VISIT to a purebred sheep show, like the All Canada Sheep Classic, which is held in a different province each year, offers a welcome relief from the mortal combat of the cow palace. Very little has changed in sheep showing circles in 75 years. All ten original breeds on the prize list at the original

What's in the Show Box?

Every competitor in the livestock classes lugs around a big wooden box containing all the tools of the trade. It's a kind of hope chest for fanatic cow lovers and it probably sits on the floor at the end of the farmer's bed. Here's what's inside:

· Electric clippers
· Halters, nose rings and leads
· Hair dryer
· Hair spray
· Shoe polish
· Shampoo, brushes, curry comb and scissors
· Registration papers, insurance, prize list
· Camera and film
· Farm brochures and business cards
· Garden hose and spray nozzle, rubber boots and rain gear
· Shirt and tie
· Molasses, which is added to the feed to make the cow look fuller
· Bloat medicine to counter the molasses after the show, kind of a pailful of bovine Tums
· Hammer, nail and fuses
· Brylcreem and gel—for the owner, not the cow
· Enamel paint spray for the hooves
· Empty coffee cups and aspirin

To properly evaluate a young sheep, a judge has to feel the fat cover and flesh around its loin.

Royal Winter Fair in 1922 are still being shown today, and some of the exhibitors look as if they might have been at that first show, too.

The Royal Winter Fair is an event with no visible means of support. The highest prize at the Royal is only $200, which might cover the cost of entry fees, stall rental and parking, but still leaves the exhibitor out of pocket for gas, the motel room out on Lakeshore Boulevard and about 15 trips to the fast-food wagon parked at the far corner of the sheep barn. Exhibitors are here for the conversation first, information second and prize money a distant third. Like their sheep, they have learned to get by on very little. Sure, there's some marketing potential in the passing crowd, but as one exhibitor says, "If that's all you came for, you're missing a lot."

The judges bend over and grip the backbone of a young animal in the market-lamb class, feeling for fat cover and flesh around the loin, which is the source of those lovely chops that are so expensive. They look at the width of his hindquarters and the squareness of his frame. Finally, the judges straighten up and announce a winner. Then they all shake hands and go for a long visit in the beer garden, where they debate weighty matters of sheep management far into the night, including whether pure-bred sheep are worth the aggravation.

Today, there are those who say that the livestock show has had its day. A totally new forum for comparing top animals is now challenging the sanctum of the show ring. The trade magazines for the beef industry now collect and publish production statistics for the leading bulls, ranking each animal for "real world" concerns such as the birth weight of his calves, their rate of gain and carcass grades. This is the sort of information a producer can flip through at home without relying on the subjective and often unexplained pronouncement of a cattle judge. Or visit the website…

Purists scoff at the idea of picking an animal out of a book or off a computer screen and warn that "you can't throw your eyeballs away." They insist it's hard to improve on the time-honoured tradition of putting the most eligible animals under the glare of hot lights and the eyes of a thousand spectators and asking a good, impartial judge to pick the best one.

Livestock shows are unlikely to disappear, because they offer an outlet for naturally gregarious and competitive people. Farming has always been a competitive business. Everyone in the old rural community joined in the same race against time and weather. A trip down the concession road told you who was ahead or behind with planting and harvest. Sleek, fat cattle grazing in the field across the road invited comparisons with your own. In that custom of comparison lies the foundation for the local fair, one of Canada's oldest and most durable forms of social organization. More than 700 of them are held between St. John's and Victoria every year. Don't miss the one nearest you.

TOM CRUICKSHANK

Best in Show

Barnyard animals have long inspired artists

WHEN A FARM family wins top honours for livestock at the Royal Winter Fair or any other agricultural event, the best way to celebrate is with a commemorative photo. Whether they know it or not, the family is maintaining a tradition that goes back a century or two, to the days before photography, when similar tributes were routinely rendered in oil portraits.

Beginning about 1800, artists would haunt country fairs in England, where they would approach the owners of prize-winning livestock to suggest a portrait. The owners were usually more than eager to oblige, but not always just to mark the occasion. In an era of illiteracy, they knew a painting was the most effective way to enhance their reputation as breeders and gain an edge over competitors. They were not above telling the artist to improve on nature by rendering the pigs fatter or the sheep woollier than, in fact, they were. It seems truth in advertising was a problem even then.

"I objected to put lumps of fat here and there where I could not see it," wrote artist Thomas Bewick (1753–1828) at the prospect of enhancing

A Prize Middle White
Sow in a Field, **painted**
by Richard Whitford, 1882

OPPOSITE: *A Flock of*
Sheep in a Barn, **painted by**
Edwin Frederick Holt, 1887.

a painting according to the customer's whim.
Today we regard such false pretensions with a
less than critical eye. In fact, some of the most
prized 19th-century animal portraits are grossly
overweight swine (above) and outrageously
shaggy sheep (opposite). They possess a naïve
charm that is the very essence of folk art.

There are equally folky treatments of horses—the exaggeration emphasizes their sheer
muscular bulk, especially when the subject is
a Shire, Belgian or other working breed—but
equine portraiture is often more sophisticated,
reflective of the status of the horse as the pride

of the traditional family farm. A good example is a circa 1910 portrait of Bramhope Romeo (below), a prize Shire stallion whose owner in Binscarth, Manitoba, hired none other than Albert Clark, progenitor of a family of animal artists of great renown in England. One of a handful of formally trained portraitists to make a living at the genre, Clark showed his stuff by ably capturing the strength of the animal without caricature.

While Romeo is solid muscle, a portrait of another Canadian horse, Martimas (opposite), shows a different approach. A famous champion whose earnings from a single race

financed a hospital wing in Hamilton, Ontario, Martimas is lean and poised. As rendered by John Sloan Gordon, an artist better known for landscapes, the pose is typical of better English horse portraits. Even the terrier is part of the English model.

The era of farm-animal portraiture came to a close in the 1920s as photo technology, especially hand-tinting and retouching, improved. There followed a sad interlude when old portraits, especially the less sophisticated folk art, were destroyed or relegated to the attic. But today these classic paintings are much admired once again—so much so that

MARTIMAS
1898

contemporary artists sometimes paint in the style of the past. Many a vintage canvas has been rescued by collectors, and some have found their way into museums. Judith James of Bolton, Ontario, is a collector-turned-curator who founded the Canadian Museum of Animal Art. She says interest in animal portraiture is burgeoning. "I sometimes wonder if it isn't the next big trend in art, much like wildlife art was in the 80s." Considering how the family farm has become an icon of nostalgia in recent years, she's probably right on the money.

Martimas, painted by John Sloan Gordon, 1898.

OPPOSITE: *Bramhope Romeo 710*, painted by Albert J. Clark, c. 1910.

Goodbye City Life!

by Tom Cruickshank

L IKE SO MANY others in her shoes (could that be you, dear reader?), Basia Halik stood at a crossroads a few years back. By any account, she had it all: a townhouse in mid-town Toronto just around the corner from her office; a wardrobe with clothing for every occasion; an active social life; and most of all, a rewarding career that did more than pay the bills. "I started fresh out of school as what they used to call a 'girl Friday,'" Basia recalls, "and worked my way up to a responsible position that took me overseas: to Brazil, Africa, Asia and Europe." Up to her neck, but never over her head, she was in the commodities business for 14 years, brokering bulk quantities of everything from tomato sauce to gherkins, apple-juice concentrate to wine, for import to Canadian foodstuffs companies. Every day presented a new challenge, but for someone as driven as Basia, it was just part of the job. But still, like the old Peggy Lee song, she found herself asking, "Is that all there is?"

Basia Halik pares her apple crop on the verandah.

"I loved my work," she says today. "I loved every day. But something was tugging at me." As fulfilling as her life was, Basia could see that the bubble might burst some day. "Maybe it was the prospect of turning 40, but I couldn't picture myself maintaining such a pace for the rest of my working life." Change was in the air, but even she didn't foresee just how different life would be in a few short months.

T HE FIRST TURNING point came in 1997 when Basia bought an 1873 stone farmhouse just outside the charming village of Neustadt, two-and-a-half hours northwest of Toronto. In the heart of German-settled farm country, the five-acre property was far removed from her workday routine. "I bought it as a weekend retreat," Basia says. And what a retreat—hidden from the road, the house abounds in old-time charm while the landscape, with unspoiled views over distant hills and dales, was the perfect tonic for a work-weary soul. "I really did my homework before I bought this place," she says, recalling the exhaustive search until she found just the right country home on just the right amount of property. She even "auditioned" her neighbours. "Before I signed on the dotted line, my boyfriend and I dropped in at a square dance, just to see how well we would blend in with the locals. We had a blast."

But if she'd done her homework before buying the house, Basia was completely unprepared for a second turning point, which came about a year later. "I up and quit my job—just like that," she relates, snapping her fingers, "and moved up here full time." It was a romantic notion, really, and in the whirlwind of selling her city house, packing her things and heading north, Basia looked forward to a new life with great enthusiasm. And then, about three weeks later, it dawned on her. She really hadn't given much thought to what she would do day to day, now that the big-city paycheque had evaporated. "I had no job, no plan and the money was going to run out fast," she says, wincing. "All of a sudden, I wondered if I had made the biggest mistake of my life."

Basia wasn't down for long. Although she had no course of action in mind, things somehow fell neatly into place. "I took a seminar and learned how to make face cream from beeswax and herbs," she says, adding that she soon had a kitchen full of face cream and nowhere to sell it.

At the same time, Basia, a born shopper, made some contacts as she explored the countryside, although "contacts" sounds

Purchased originally as a weekend retreat, this 1873 stone farmhouse became Basia's permanent residence just one year later.

more professional than it really was. "I discovered which apiary made the best honey, where to find the best local maple syrup, which artisan made the best homemade soap and where to find artistic dried-flower arrangements," she continues. "I suppose it was just a matter of time before I opened a retail shop where all this stuff could be sold."

AT FIRST, STOREKEEPING seemed like nothing more than a fleeting thought, but as she gave it more consideration, Basia decided it wasn't such a long shot. "Neustadt isn't a tourist destination, but it gets lots of traffic on weekends—mostly cottagers from London and Kitchener in the south headed toward the beaches of Lake Huron and Georgian Bay in the

Garden at a Glance

LOCATION: On five acres severed from original 300-acre dairy farm. Near Neustadt, Ontario, about 93 miles (150 km) north of Toronto, on the way to Owen Sound.

ZONE: On the cusp between 5A and 5B, one of the cooler spots in western Ontario. Higher and more exposed than surrounding townships, the area is subject to extreme summer storms and lake-effect snow off Lake Huron.

SOIL: Typical southern Ontario clay-loam with plenty of glacial till thrown in for good measure. Gardens augmented with heaping helpings of peat moss and well-rotted sheep manure.

WATER: Steady rainfall means that drought is rarely a problem. Even so, a cistern is at the ready when rains fail.

PHILOSOPHY: There's really no pattern or plan to the garden. Beds evolve based on location and available sunlight, and according to garden plots left behind by former owners. If there's one guiding principle, it is to preserve the down-home rural character of the house and yard.

Basia's five-acre plot of land, just outside Neustadt, offers enough room to grow vegetables, fruit, herbs and flowers, and raise chickens.

north." As the wheels were turning, she saw a "For Rent" sign in the window of a main-street shop and ever since, Basia's "Harvest Room" has been selling a cornucopia of local wares, including new batches of Basia's face cream.

The shop was a first for Neustadt, whose retail sector seemed to be losing the battle with Hanover, Walkerton and other larger towns in the area. But the Harvest Room seems to have ushered in a new era, as it has since been joined by a handful of other boutiques, galleries and a bistro, all catering to an out-of-town clientele. Even the local brewery, housed in a handsome century-old stone building that had been closed for decades, is making beer once again. Indeed, Neustadt has turned a corner—it has even been cited in *Harrowsmith Country Life* as one of the

Basia likes to work with dried hydrangea and other floral stems. Her decorative work is on view at her Harvest Room boutique.

Few chickens have it as good as Basia's. Not only does she allow her Aracaunas and Rhode Island Reds the run of the backyard, they reside in an insulated and heated former children's playhouse.

Basia inherited an apple orchard when she bought the property and augmented the grove with selections of plum and cherry trees.

prettiest villages in Canada. "Here, I certainly don't have the big salary I once did," Basia says of her new venture, "but it's been fun to see my ideas take shape."

Meanwhile, back at her new homestead, Basia embarked on any number of projects, admitting that she was a hopeless greenhorn at first. "Let me tell you about the calamities of a city woman who hardly knew a cistern from a well at the time," she recalls, thinking back to the appalling number of occasions she had to be towed out of the snow banks that line her quarter-mile driveway. Or the time the wind blew the latch shut and she was locked inside her chicken coop—"I had to wiggle out the window."

At times, Basia wondered why she ever expected to make a new life in such an unfamiliar environment, but maybe that's just the point. "To this day, I can't quite explain why or how I made the move," she says. After all, she is the daughter of immigrant Polish parents who settled in the blue-collar town of Oshawa after World War II. "It's not as though rural Ontario was in my blood." But she has managed to triumph against the odds and perhaps that is as big a reward as any city job could ever have offered.

Even so, Basia admits that it was almost foolhardy to quit the city on such a whim. "But it was the only way," she reasons now. "If I had waited until I'd found the right job up here or until I'd saved enough money, I may never have had the courage, and I'd still be living and working in Toronto." Food for thought for all you city-bound readers, isn't it?

KARYN WOODLAND

A Dog's Life

The exciting world of sheepdog trials

I T IS THE dog's instinct to chase and the sheep's to run. Back in the old days, not so long ago, a farmer with a flock would prize any dog with a talent for herding, an inbred ability to keep his charges together and guide them back to the barn. A good shepherd dog is still an asset on the farm, but nowadays, herding is more for sport than survival. The sport is called trialing and provides a unique competition for clever canines, usually border collies, to test their mettle with the skittish sheep.

A sheepdog trial is a fascinating thing to watch. While a novice dog may get too excited to perform well, a seasoned pro works the flock like a choreographer. Aware that spooked sheep will scatter unpredictably, a champion doesn't so much drive the sheep as nudge them along, all the while listening for verbal commands or whistles from his master. Remaining at a designated post, the crook-bearing handler sends the dog to the top of the field to fetch a flock of five, and then escort it back through gates and into a pen. Timing is key: If the dog approaches too quickly, the sheep disperse; too slowly, and time runs out. The trial judge scores the dogs on their expertise in marshalling the sheep through the course within the seven-minute limit. The pros (three years and older) get another 90 seconds to separate the flock into two groups.

"It's a thrill to watch a young dog discover how it can influence and control livestock," enthuses Aileen McConnell, a retired doctor turned sheep farmer. "It sends shivers up

A border collie's work is never done. Just ask Bob Stephens, shown above with "Turk."

your spine to see that amount of knowledge, intensity and power—and be part of that team." With support from local farmers, she and fellow border collie enthusiast Martha McHardy run the Metchosin sheepdog trials. Sheep are still important to this Vancouver Island town, just west of Victoria, which makes it a natural for trialing. Every July, about 40 handlers and 50 dogs come from all over western Canada and the U.S. Pacific northwest to compete. "We have this combination of

lovely, big fields and 300 available sheep," says McConnell, of the incentive for the trials. "How could we not do it?"

One of only two events on Vancouver Island, the trials are sanctioned by the U.S. Border Collie Handlers' Association, the B.C. Stock Dog Association (BCSDA), and the Oregon Sheep Dog Society. Winners get nice ribbons and some cash, but the real trophies are the points they accumulate, which can help secure an entry into the big-name competitions, like the American finals.

The vast majority of competitors are border collies, a highly disciplined breed known for their high IQs. Never content to sit still, these smart dogs long ago stole the limelight from other herding dogs, such as German shepherds and Old English sheepdogs. "Though great competitors, border collies don't always make

great pets," says McConnell. "They're working dogs and are always busy. If you don't find something for them to do, they'll usually find it themselves."

To the average person, they look like a Heinz 57, but the border collie is not your average dog. One of the most energetic canines on the planet, their herding instinct is legendary. "They live to work and are eager to please," says one aficionado. Unlike some breeds, looks aren't a major concern. No one cares if ears are perky or floppy; coats may be long or short. Likewise, colour is irrelevant, although black and white is traditional. What matters most is the combination of intelligence, agility and a willingness to learn.

The border collie earned its reputation in the highlands of Wales and Scotland, a godsend to shepherds keeping watch over vast flocks of

Marshalling sheep followed by some welcome affection—does a dog need more?

sheep. The dogs also proved adept at herding cattle, pigs and goats. With a general decline in sheep farming, border collies are kept busy these days shooing Canada geese from golf courses and, of course, in the sport of trialing. Meanwhile, their intelligence has caught the attention of wilderness search-and-rescue teams. They know a smart dog when they see one.

"These dogs are bred for their brains," confirms former-BCSDA president Bob Stephens. A retired RCMP dog master, Stephens raises sheep and border collies on his property near Kamloops; that is, when he isn't on the trialing circuit. "Fan," his two-year-old competitor, took the nursery category (under three years) in Metchosin in 2002.

Stephens also ran nine-year-old "Del'mar Turk" in the pro division that year. But Turk was a tad too "fired up" from two big wins the previous week in Penticton and at the Calgary Stampede to impress the judges in Metchosin. At the Stampede, competing with 71 other dogs in the trials called the "$hoot Out" with a four-minute time limit, Turk took the $10,000 prize money in one minute eight seconds. "The dogs always have to come down off these highs," Stephens explained. "They get into a power trip, so much that they're hard to control."

Turk and Nan are now retired, but Bob and his wife Nancy continue to compete with their offspring. "Wisp" ran in the World Sheep Dog Trial in Tullamore, Ireland in 2005, and his brother "Ike" came in second at the Canadian National Championships in Kingston, Ontario in 2004. Success is obviously in their genes.

Tomatoes for Tomorrow

by Darlene King

THERE ARE LOTS of reasons to collect the seeds from this year's crop of tomatoes. Perhaps the name of a particularly successful variety eludes you, but you still have the evidence on the vine. Perhaps there's no other choice, especially if you've lucked into some heirloom tomato long discontinued from the mainstream seed catalogues. Or perhaps you just want the satisfaction of nurturing a crop from start to finish.

Whatever the reason, collecting seeds is hardly rocket science. The trick is that the tomato is not like other vegetables, in that the seeds are surrounded by a gelatinous coating. This sac prevents the seeds from germinating inside the tomato, and must be removed (see Step 3 on the following page) before the seeds can be dried and stored.

Saving the seeds from a tomato variety you like ensures a good supply the next season.

STEP 1 Harvest

Gather the best tomatoes from your garden. Choose only from the strongest plants, those that produced the greatest yield and the tastiest fruit. Above all, select specimens that withstood disease and drought. For best results, pick when slightly overripe.

STEP 2 Remove the Seeds

Cut the tomatoes in half and gently squeeze out the seeds, including the gelatinous sac, into a glass jar (a).

STEP 3 Ferment the Seeds

For the seeds to sprout next spring, you'll have to separate them from the gel through fermentation. This will also destroy many seed-borne bacterial diseases. To get the process under way, add as much water to the jar as you have seeds and juice. Do not cover, even though you may be tempted to do so if an odour develops. Place the jar in the basement or some other out-of-the-way place. Keep it at room temperature for three or four days.

STEP 4 Remove the Mould

At the end of the fermentation period, you will find a fuzzy layer of mould on the surface of the tomato and water mixture. This is not cause for alarm. Simply remove it with a spoon. Add a little water and stir vigorously to remove any traces of mould that might remain. Ladle out any stray pulp or debris.

STEP 5 Collect the Seeds

The viable seeds will settle to the bottom of the jar. Spoon off any seeds that rise to the top. Sieve the mixture through a fine strainer and collect the viable seeds (b). If debris remains on the seeds, put them back in the jar and add a little more water to rinse the seeds again. Pour them back through the strainer until only clean seeds remain.

STEP 6 Dry the Seeds

Sprinkle the viable seeds into a bowl and allow them to air-dry. Over the next few days, stir them with your finger on occasion to ensure they dry completely (c). Store in an envelope and keep them in a cool, dry place until ready to plant next year.

DAN NEEDLES

Country Etiquette

True confessions from the Ninth Concession

IT MUST BE DAUNTING for a city person to land in a place like Nottawasaga Township and try to make sense of the language, rituals and taboos of rural life. Like Humphrey Bogart, that person might feel that the rest of the world was three drinks behind. As a transplant myself, I think I am qualified to act as a kind of Etienne Brulé to the newly arrived Champlains, and guide newcomers around with a few useful tips on country etiquette.

The first rule, of course, is to be careful what you say about people because they're all related.

In the country, lunch is the meal served at a funeral or at midnight after a dance. The meal in the middle of the day is called dinner and the evening meal is called supper. If you cross the threshold of someone's home at any of these times, you're invited in to eat. If you feel the urge to reciprocate, this is good, but forget the city custom of inviting people over for cocktails and throwing them out with nothing to eat. This is more than puzzling to a country person, and it conflicts sharply with their views about hospitality.

It's fine to talk crops, but be careful not to say anything that might be taken as criticism. A careless remark about weeds will hang in the air for years. On the other hand, don't enthuse about a crop that is still in the ground because this might bring bad luck. Obviously, this leaves a very narrow window of opportunity for small talk about crops, which is why the farmers themselves chat with each other in such mind-numbing technical detail about corn heat units and herbicide rates, or simply move on to the weather.

The Japanese tea ceremony is an uncomplicated affair compared to the ritual of the rural wave, which entails knowing when to wave, how often to wave in the same day, whether to engage the arm at the shoulder, elbow or wrist and when the simple straightening of one index finger on the steering wheel will do.

When city people arrive, the first thing they do is slap up some "No Trespassing" signs around their property. All these signs ever do is persuade your neighbours that you are haughty and remote. Trespassers and messy picnickers can be controlled with a sign that says "Beware of Snakes." But in time you will learn, as I have, that a figure walking across your field is more of a reason to put the kettle on than to call the police.

The country was made for visiting. Rail fences and pickup truck boxes are designed at just the right height so you can put your elbows over them, lean and yarn with a neighbour for an hour or so. The diner in the village is the sort of restaurant where you don't look for a table, you just find a chair.

None of this is coincidence. The old rural community was built on an elaborate system of shared work and play that revolved around a seasonal timetable and was knit together by visits and stories. Evidence of that old code still appears in the speech and manners of residents in the same way old barn foundations poke through the landscape. And the great irony is that, as society restructures around home-based occupations and more people return to the sideroads to rebuild on the old foundations, they find themselves rediscovering the ancient art of neighbouring.

> A figure walking across your field is more of a reason to put the kettle on than to call the police.

A Taste of Autumn

by Darlene King

Medley of Three Squash Soup

Don't tell anyone who doesn't like squash what's in this soup—they'll never guess. Try any combination of squashes, although one variety will certainly suffice. This soup stores well and can be made a day ahead.

MAKES 8 CUPS (SERVES 6)

½ lb	butternut squash	220 g
½ lb	acorn squash	220 g
½ lb	hubbard or turban squash	220 g
1 Tbsp	olive oil	15 ml
1	small onion, chopped	1
1 lb	carrots, peeled and thinly sliced	450 g
1 tsp	paprika	5 ml
2 tsp	ground cumin	10 ml
2 tsp	ground coriander	10 ml
1 tsp	turmeric	5 ml
1	clove garlic, finely minced	1
4 cups	chicken stock	1 l
	salt and pepper	
	plain yogurt	
	cilantro leaves	

Cut squash into large pieces and discard seeds. Bake in 350°F (180°C) oven until tender, about 45 minutes to 1 hour.

Gently heat olive oil. Add chopped onion and carrot and sauté until onion is translucent. Stir in spices and garlic and cook for one minute longer. Add stock. Scoop out baked squash from shells and stir into stock mixture.

Bring soup to boil and gently simmer, covered, until carrots are tender, approximately 30 minutes. Remove from heat. Purée soup in a blender or food processor until very smooth. Strain into a clean saucepan, season with salt and pepper and thin with a little more stock if too thick.

Serve with a dollop of plain yogurt and garnish with cilantro.

Butternut Squash Pasta
with Zucchini and Lemon

PASTA DOUGH

¾ cup	butternut squash, peeled and cubed	180 ml
2	eggs	2
½ Tbsp	olive oil	7.5 ml
2¼ cups	all-purpose flour	540 ml
¼ tsp	salt	1.2 ml
¼ tsp	cayenne pepper	1.2 ml
	freshly ground black pepper	

ZUCCHINI AND LEMON SAUCE

½ cup	dry white wine	120 ml
¼ tsp	saffron threads	1.2 ml
2 Tbsp	olive oil	30 ml
2	medium zucchini, cut in julienne strips	2
	salt and pepper	
1 Tbsp	butter	15 ml
3	large shallots, sliced thin	3
2	cloves garlic, finely minced	2
1 cup	chicken stock	240 ml
½ cup	heavy cream, 35%	120 ml
2 tsp	grated lemon zest	20 ml
¼ cup	grated parmesan cheese	60 ml

PART OF the fun of preparing this creative dish is making homemade pasta, a task made easier if you have a pasta machine for rolling out the dough. This tasty entrée calls for zucchini as well as winter squash. The presentation looks especially pleasing with the yellow-gold of the pasta and the green stripes of the zucchini.

Place cubed squash in small saucepan of lightly salted, boiling water. Boil for 10 minutes or until tender. Drain well and cool.

Combine cooled squash and eggs in a food processor and pulse until just combined. Add olive oil, flour, salt and cayenne pepper. Combine just until sticky and blended. Remove mixture from processor and knead with flour until a soft ball is formed. Dough should be slightly sticky. Let rest 1 hour.

Cut dough into four pieces. Flour first piece lightly. Roll dough through largest setting on pasta machine. Fold pasta into three, flour and pass through same setting twice more. Continue to pass dough through machine decreasing settings until pasta reaches desired thickness (second last setting on pasta machine). Lay dough on a countertop, and grind black pepper on top and pat it into dough before passing through machine a final time. Cut through fettuccine cutter on machine. Hang to dry.

To make pasta by hand, combine cooled squash and eggs in separate bowl. Mix well. Sift flour, salt and cayenne pepper onto work surface. Make a well in centre of flour mixture and add squash mixture and oil. Blend by hand. Knead until dough forms a soft ball and is still slightly sticky. Let pasta rest for 1 hour.

Roll out pasta by hand with a rolling pin on a well-floured surface to desired thickness (approximately ⅛″). Before cutting into strips, grind black pepper all over dough. Roll a little more, making sure all pepper is rolled into dough. Cut into strips with pizza cutter and hang to dry.

Bring a large pot of salted water to boil.

ZUCCHINI AND LEMON SAUCE

In a small saucepan, warm wine over low heat. Remove from heat and add saffron. Set aside.

Heat olive oil in a large skillet. Add zucchini and sauté until it starts to brown. Transfer to a plate and season with salt and pepper. Keep warm.

In same skillet, melt butter. Add shallots and sauté over medium heat until translucent, approximately 4 minutes.

Add garlic and sauté one minute. Raise heat and pour in wine and stock. Bring to a boil and reduce by half. Pour in cream and reduce by half again. Add lemon zest and season with salt and pepper.

Add pasta to boiling water and cook until just tender, about 3 to 5 minutes for fresh pasta. Drain and return to pot. Add sauce and toss. Transfer to a pasta bowl, sprinkle with parmesan cheese and half the zucchini and toss gently. Top with reserved zucchini and serve.

Apple Cranberry Pie
with Oatmeal Walnut Topping

CRUST

1 cup	all-purpose flour	240 ml
2 Tbsp	firmly packed golden brown sugar	30 ml
½ tsp	salt	2.5 ml
¼ cup	unsalted butter	60 ml
¼ cup	solid vegetable shortening	60 ml
¼ cup	rolled oats	60 ml
¼ tsp	ground cinnamon	1.2 ml
¼ tsp	ground nutmeg	1.2 ml
1 Tbsp	water	15 ml

FILLING

2 lbs	apples peeled, cored, sliced thin	1 kg
½ cup	cranberries, fresh or frozen, thawed	120 ml
1 Tbsp	all-purpose flour	15 ml
1 tsp	ground cinnamon	5 ml
1 tsp	ground nutmeg	5 ml
2 tsp	butter	10 ml
½ cup	sugar	120 ml

TOPPING

½ cup	all purpose flour	120 ml
¼ cup	firmly packed golden brown sugar	60 ml
1 tsp	cinnamon	5 ml
½ tsp	ground nutmeg	2.5 ml
2 tsp	unsalted butter cut into pieces	30 ml
½ cup	rolled oats	120 ml
3 Tbsp	chopped walnuts	45 ml

Two FALL flavours—apples and cranberries—combine to make this mouth-watering dessert. Serve warm with a scoop of vanilla ice cream for a real treat.

CRUST

In a mixing bowl or food processor, combine flour, sugar, salt, cinnamon, nutmeg. Then add butter and shortening until mixture resembles coarse meal. Add rolled oats, pulse to blend. Mix in water. Blend until moist clumps form. Gather dough into bowl, flatten into disks, wrap in plastic wrap. Refrigerate for at least 30 minutes. (Can be stored in fridge for at least 3 days. Let dough soften slightly before continuing.)

FILLING

Preheat oven to 375°F (190°C). Combine all ingredients in a bowl and toss well.

TOPPING

Place the flour, brown sugar, cinnamon, nutmeg, salt and butter in the bowl of a food processor. Pulse until the mixture forms small clumps. Mix in the oats and walnuts just until combined. Set aside while assembling the pie.

To assemble the pie:

Roll the pie dough between two pieces of wax paper to form an 11-inch (27 cm) circle. Peel off the top sheet of paper. Invert the dough into a 9-inch (23 cm) pie plate. The dough is cookie-like so it may break apart. Repair any holes with patches of dough. Fold, edge and crimp the crust decoratively. Spoon the filling into the crust. Sprinkle the topping over the filling.

Place in the oven and bake for 35 to 45 minutes. If the top begins to brown too quickly, cover the top of the pie lightly with aluminum foil. Steam must still be able to escape. The pie can be made 2 days ahead. Reheat before serving.

winter

winter musings

EARLY INTO YOUR move to the country—perhaps about the beginning of March, when yet another blizzard is raging and all that remain in the cold cellar are a few leathery carrots and some questionable potatoes—you're apt to pause to ponder what life would have been like for our ancestors. They were the original country dwellers, the early settlers who felled the forests and eked a living from the land. Like us several generations later, many of them were city-raised and lacking in basic homesteading skills, but 150 years ago, the stakes were much higher. Indeed, the storm that would be a mere inconvenience today could easily have brought the countryside to a standstill back then. And those meagre cellar vegetables would have looked mighty tempting in an era with no supermarkets. So when winter feels like it will never end, all you have to do to lift your spirits is cast a thought back to bygone days. No matter how dreary the season can get, it could only have been worse for our forebears.

However, this notion of the past is largely a misconception, at least once the 19th-century rural community had established itself. For them—a generation raised on the farm and long past subsistence living—there was more to winter than simply waiting out the bad weather. The colder months were the time of year that offered the most leisure hours and, traditionally, farm folk spent much of the time socializing and indulging in such seasonal pursuits as tobogganing and curling. There's a lesson for us here: It seems that if you're well enough prepared, with the shed full of firewood and the pantry shelves stacked high with preserves, winter need not be so oppressive after all.

At *Harrowsmith Country Life*, we learned a long time ago that winter is also an occasion for contemplation and planning anew. Sitting by the fire, there's no better time for garden enthusiasts to muse about the year to come as they pore over a new crop of nursery and seed catalogues. And likewise, winter is the season in which new projects are hatched: Vegetable gardens are planned, fence lines are plotted and if there's a new hobby on the horizon—livestock, maple syrup—now is the time to get organized. See what we mean as you browse the pages that follow.

If you have any doubts about moving to the country, your first winter will make or break you. You will either emerge triumphant, confident that you made the right decision, or you will be hammering the "for sale" sign into the front lawn as soon as the ground thaws. But don't make up your mind until you've at least tried your hand at boiling your own maple syrup. Even the most un-handyman can do it and once you've tasted that sweet elixir of the hardwood forest, wrought by your own labour, you'll understand why you moved to the country in the first place. Indeed, no stale carrot nor late-winter blizzard will be able to ruin your day.

Ram-ifications

by Tom Cruickshank

IT'S PROBABLY A foreign concept to you and, only a few years ago, rammed earth construction was, likewise, an unknown quantity to Mark Haughey and Brenda Plaxton. At the time, the couple—newly arrived urban refugees from Calgary—was considering any number of alternative building techniques for their new house on Salt Spring Island, British Columbia, and although it was uncharted territory, something about using dirt—basic, unadulterated earth—as a building material struck a chord. "Perhaps it's because of my background as a geologist," Mark muses. Eager to build a house that reflected his environmental ethic, rammed earth appealed most to him, even more than straw bale, cob, stack-wall or other out-of-the-mainstream building materials.

Rammed earth houses are known for their organic appeal and Brenda Plaxton and Mark Haughey's house is no exception. It was designed to blend effortlessly with its environment.

Brenda approached it from a different angle. After a bout with environmental allergies that had sent her to the hospital, she vowed that her next home would be free of mould, dust and household contaminants that can render a dwelling uncomfortable, if not uninhabitable. "Rammed earth houses have a reputation for good indoor air quality," she remarks. There is very little wood in them—only a fraction of what would be used in a conventional frame house—and hence, fewer opportunities for mould to grow, which is often the culprit behind the foul indoor air. Nor do they contain any of a whole list of chemicals—fungicides, solvents, and formaldehyde—that are routinely found in conventional construction materials.

Although new to this country, rammed earth is one of the oldest construction methods in the world. Its basic component is ordinary dirt, mixed with a measure of water, a dash of cement and soupçon of pigment. It doesn't sound like much to base a building on, but when dumped into forms, layer upon layer of the earth mixture is "rammed"—that is, pummelled and pounded and tamped and battered—until it morphs into something as hard and as durable as concrete. Removing the forms reveals an earthen wall that is as beautiful as it is strong. "I love the look of a rammed earth wall," Mark says. There are subtle striations in colour and variations in texture—here and there, you can discern the layers—which lends a unique and natural appearance lacking in, say, factory brick or ordinary poured concrete. "Even on the interior, rammed earth is designed to be seen," he says. And, uninhibited by convention, the technique lends itself to innovative, free-flowing architectural statements—indeed, rammed earth houses are guaranteed to turn heads.

BRENDA AND MARK were introduced to the concept through Meror Krayenhoff, a local contractor with a keen interest in eco-building and sustainable living. It was he who brought rammed earth to Salt Spring—indeed, his company, Terra Firma Builders Ltd. was the first to bring it to Canada, after he studied buildings in the Middle East and Australia. Brenda and Mark's house is his 12th rammed earth project. "Aesthetics are important," he says, "but only the beginning of the long list of the virtues of earth buildings." For example, rammed earth houses are so solid that they boast superb acoustics and rank with the best in terms of fire resistance. They also score points for exceptionally low maintenance. "There is no siding to repair

Rammed earth walls have subtle variations in colour.

Mark and Brenda take five on the patio of their ocean-side home on Salt Spring Island.

and no painting to be done. And because it doesn't rely on wood, the structure will never rot, nor will it be host to carpenter ants or termites, which are the scourge of stick-frame buildings, especially out here on the coast." In the long run, Meror believes this more than compensates for the premium—about 15 percent over ordinary dwellings—in up-front costs.

The dearth of wood is another factor in rammed earth's favour. "It doesn't require much lumber," Meror continues, noting that conventional homes consume about 47 trees each. "We use dirt instead of wood—that's a big environmental bonus." But its biggest trump card, according to Meror, lies in energy efficiency, specifically thermal mass, which has long been acknowledged as a major factor in passive solar applications. "To take advantage of

Anatomy of a Rammed Earth Wall

A Rubble trench—4-inch (10 cm) bed of drain rock

B Reinforced concrete footing—up to 5 feet (1.5 m) wide

C PVC drain pipe

D Interior rammed earth wall, reinforced with steel rebar

E 4″ (10 cm) foam insulation

F Exterior rammed earth wall, reinforced with steel rebar

G Carpet-tube or PVC pipe to function as electrical conduit

H Wooden top plate, anchored to wall, ready for roof truss

I Interior floor

J Acrylic coating on all exposed earth surface to inhibit dust

S.I.R.E.—Stabilized Insulated Rammed Earth Wall

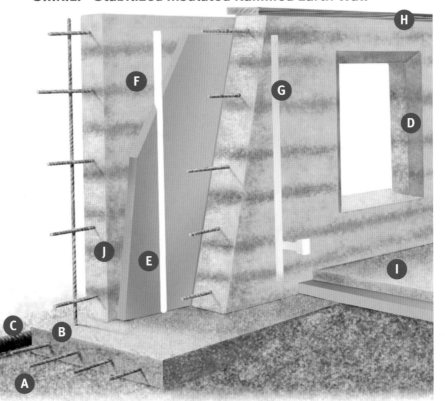

the natural warmth of the sun, you need a large, solid-as-a-rock surface that can absorb a lot of heat and store it. Concrete and stone masonry are often cited as prime materials for thermal mass, but my technique, with solid earth walls up to 24 inches (61 cm) thick, is certainly in the same ball park," he says.

Even so, Meror saw room for improvement. He says that rammed earth works like a charm in a warm climate, but in Canada—even in a place as balmy as Salt Spring—its thermal capabilities need a helping hand. So Meror went the concept one better by embedding a layer of rigid insulation within his walls. "This boosts their thermal performance to at least R33, which is more than adequate to weather a Canadian winter," he says. But the innovations didn't stop there. Meror also saw room for improvement when it came to seismic issues—an often overlooked, but very real concern on the west coast. "Here, it's important that a building stands a fighting chance in the event of an earthquake," so he bolsters all his installations with steel reinforcing bars, placed at regular intervals. Together, the two innovations—thermal and seismic—mark Meror's work as uniquely suited to local conditions: A cut above, he calls it the "S.I.R.E." for Stabilized Insulated Rammed Earth wall.

Rammed Earth Comes to Canada

EVEN IF YOU'VE never heard the official name before, you're probably already familiar with rammed earth houses. Anyone who has admired a postcard view of a quaint Mediterranean port has seen them—a jumble of whitewashed houses with red tile roofs climbing the seaside hills. Indeed, they have been the standard in house construction in southern Europe and the Middle East since biblical times. None other than the Great Wall of China, or at least most of it, was built of rammed earth. Today, it is still the basic building material through much of the world and although rooted in tradition, it has easily adapted to modern architecture. More than just for houses, many a mall, school and hospital in Western Australia—indeed, 20 percent of all local construction—is made of rammed earth. Meanwhile, the Perth yellow pages are chock full of rammed earth contractors.

But it's a long way from sunny Australia to the Great White North. Meror Krayenhoff's foray into rammed earth construction was the first—and still one of the few—attempts to introduce the technology to Canada. With all its attributes, you'd think it would have caught on like the hula-hoop, but so far, rammed earth houses are as rare as a smiling face on Bay Street.

Meror says it's all a matter of what we're used to. "Rammed earth evolved in hot, dry climates, where wood is too rare and precious to be used as a building

Developed in hot climates where wood is rare, rammed earth is also suitable for the colder temperatures of a northern winter.

material," he says. Meanwhile, the Canadian building tradition is the exact opposite—stick-frame construction is so ingrained that anything else is greeted with raised eyebrows." Indeed, rammed earth has yet to be recognized in local building codes and there is some scepticism, even among environmentalists, that it is practical anywhere but Salt Spring and environs, whose winters are hardly as severe as the Canadian norm. Meror scoffs at doubters. "There is a long tradition of rammed earth in the French Alps," he says, and he knows of experiments with the technique in Yukon. "I think rammed earth has great possibilities in less temperate parts of the country," he continues. Currently, Meror is

proving his point as work proceeds on his current project, a rammed earth nature interpretive centre for the Osoyoos First Nation in the British Columbia interior. From there, he's anxious to apply his technique to an even colder locale.

For anyone considering the merits of rammed earth building, Meror Krayenhoff offers enlightening weekend seminars on Salt Spring Island. Participants learn the basics of the technique, tour several local rammed earth houses and even get to do a little on-site ramming. Check www.sirewall.com for dates, fees and more information.

High on the list of priorities was Brenda and Mark's desire to take advantage of every view to the water.

THE MORE BRENDA and Mark learned, the more they were convinced that rammed earth would work for them. "In 2000, we started bouncing ideas around," Brenda recalls. "We left the technical stuff to Meror and relied on his creative staff, notably staff designer Ron Cooke, to shape concepts into a firm plan." From the start, the couple had some basic criteria in mind: that the architecture blend with its surroundings; that all amenities be on one floor; and most of all, that the principal rooms, especially the master suite and living area, take advantage of the available view. And what a view: a typical Salt Spring vista over the Strait of Georgia. "The best vantage point was from a spot close to the shore where previous owners had built a small cabin," Brenda continues. Without a second thought, the cabin was sold and towed to a new location, leaving the site clear for their new home.

It took a long time to work out a floor plan—that's the nature of rammed earth, because all the mechanical systems, such as plumbing and wiring, have to be settled precisely beforehand since they will be buried within the earth walls. Construction finally commenced in the summer of 2003, and Mark and Brenda were always on hand to watch the progress. "A pad was cleared in the middle of the yard to function as a palette on which the basic building ingredients—the soil, water, cement and pigment—were mixed together," Mark says. To get an artistic variation in colour now and then, the amount of pigment in the recipe would vary somewhat. "When the mixture had the right consistency—it should crumble like cookie dough—a skid-steer would pour the earth into the forms." But Mark was more than a mere observer. Putting his regular nine-to-five routine aside for the duration, he donned a hard hat and became one of the crew, more than willing to climb into the wall-forms with a pneumatic compressor and help with the ramming. "All that pounding, hours of it, is very labour intensive," Mark recalls. "It took two whole months, but it was well worth it." Not only did his own labour save significantly on the bottom line, he was also proud to have had a hand in building his own house. "How many other people can say that?" he beams.

State-of-the-art creature comforts—notably in the kitchen—add to the appeal of the home.

Now that the house is completed, Mark and Brenda can bask in the pride of a job well done. "Only this past December, during our very first winter here, the house earned its stripes," Brenda says, recalling an anomalous snowstorm that plunged Salt Spring into a prolonged blackout. "After three days without heat and electricity, our neighbours were bailing out, while our rammed earth walls kept us tolerably warm."

Mark concurs. "That storm confirmed that we had done the right thing," he says. "Not only did we build the house of our dreams, we also built something that satisfies our environmental conscience." No longer is rammed earth a foreign concept for Mark and Brenda—no doubt, they'll be singing its praises for years to come.

The Recipe

SUBSOIL:

10 parts. Do not use topsoil.

WATER:

1 part

CEMENT:

1 part

PIGMENT:

0.2 to 0.6 parts

FORUMULA:

The formula for rammed earth varies, especially by colour—it can vary from chocolate brown through all shades of earth tones to muted beige—but the basic recipe starts and ends with plain old dirt. It has been compared to both concrete and adobe brick, but it definitely isn't.

NOT ADOBE:

Similar to rammed earth in that its basic ingredient is earth, adobe differs because it is formed into blocks, which are not assembled in place until they are dried in the sun.

NOT CONCRETE:

Like concrete, rammed earth is poured into forms. However, concrete employs gravel and sand, not earth, and much more water. It is also more demanding of resources.

1

2

3

1 As if the ground were a mixing bowl and the skid-steer bucket a Mixmaster, the essential ingredients—earth, cement and pigment—are stirred and blended together.

2 Water is added to the dry components until the recipe acquires the texture of cookie dough. If a clump shatters when tossed to the ground, it's just the right consistency.

3 Its bucket full of the raw, mixed ingredients, the skid-steer heads over to the house site, where the

wall forms stand at the ready. The earth is then dumped into the form.

4 Then the ramming begins. Homeowner Mark climbs into the form with his pneumatic compressing tool and rams the earth…and rams it…and rams it…

5 …and rams it some more until the earth is pounded hard and firm. As the wall is filled up with earth, new sections are added to the form until the wall reaches its full height. Forms are left in place until the work has a chance to dry.

6 With the forms removed, the wall stands in all its glory. Subtle striations and variations in colour—signatures of rammed earth construction—mark the numerous rammed layers. The free-form architecture is beginning to materialize as most of the walls stand in place. The foreground will be filled in with yet more walls.

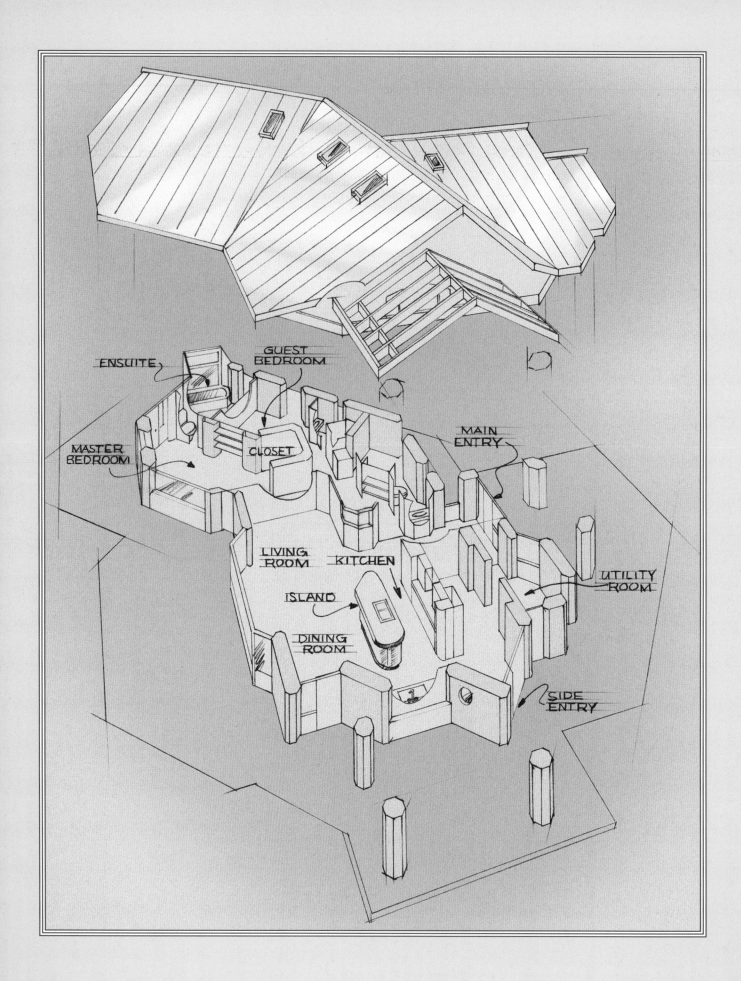

ENSUITE

GUEST
BEDROOM

MASTER
BEDROOM

CLOSET

MAIN
ENTRY

LIVING
ROOM

KITCHEN

UTILITY
ROOM

ISLAND

DINING
ROOM

SIDE
ENTRY

Specs

CONCEPT: New single-storey home on oceanfront 4-acre lot. Employs unusual rammed-earth construction technique. Design and construction: Meror Krayenhoff and Ron Cooke, Terra Firma Builders, Salt Spring Island, British Columbia.

GENESIS: Construction under way September 2003; occupied December 2004.

LOCATION: Salt Spring Island, B.C.

BEDROOMS: 2

BATHROOMS: 3

TOTAL USABLE FLOOR AREA: about 2,300 square feet (214 m²) on one level.

CONSTRUCTION: Rammed earth employs soil as a building material, which is poured into forms and compressed into solid walls. Special seismic adaptation and added insulation by builder.

FOUNDATION: For seismic stability, the structure requires extra-wide (five to six feet) (1.5 m) concrete footings.

ROOF: Metal standing-seam panels. Chosen for its environmental capabilities, the roof will last longer than other roofing materials and can be recycled. Rainwater is collected from roof and stored for household use.

INSULATION: Rigid foam insulation integrated into earth walls (see illustration, page 192); icynene spray-foam in ceilings.

ELECTRICAL SERVICE: Standard 200-amp service.

HEAT: Water-source heat pump extracts warmth from seawater and stores it for household use in a heat exchanger. Considered an exceptionally eco-friendly type of home heat in that, except for a small amount of electricity to run the unit, it does not rely on fossil fuels. Heat dispensed through rooms via radiant-floor cables.

WINDOWS: Low-E, double-glazed, argon-filled units—aluminum cladding over wood frames.

FLOORS: Poured concrete, tinted with pigment.

Everybody Must Get Stones

by John Shaw-Rimmington

U P ON BALSAM Lake in Ontario's cottage country and down in Prince Edward County—and here and there in other parts of Canada—the rural landscape is lined with miles of dry stone walls. Built of rubble collected from the fields and assembled without benefit of any kind of mortar, they have been standing for generations with only gravity to hold them together. In an era that prides itself on industrial technology, they seem an anomaly. Indeed, they are—and therein lies their charm.

This dry stone wall built by stone mason John Shaw-Rimmington features a turf top.

Dry stone walls are a rural tradition that goes back to the British Isles. Traditionally, a land in which wood was too precious to use for fencing, stone was free for the taking, and the logical medium for dividing farm fields. More than just a random pile of boulders, dry stone walls evolved into an art form that is as brilliant as it is simple. By packing the walls tight, by making sure that every stone is secure against another, and by ensuring that the wall tapers toward the top, the work is amazingly solid and stands the test of time. Unlike a wooden fence or a hedge, it requires next to no maintenance—except perhaps every decade or so, you might have to realign a few stones.

L IKE SO MANY other rural skills—from cheese-making to timber-framing—the craft of dry stone walling lapsed through much of the 20th century, only to be reborn recently by a corps of enthusiasts keen on its revival. They see folk art in the thoughtful placement of stones and the desire to master the skill of fitting stones in traditional applications. They work with stone structurally, not merely as a veneer or decoration. But you don't have to be an experienced stonemason to build a dry stone wall. Although it demands a strong back—a large stone can weigh up to 100 pounds (45 kg)– it requires no special tools and the basic skill is easy to learn Even if you've never built anything before, you can get satisfactory results with just a little practice.

Walling does demand perseverance, however. A novice builder is lucky to complete four feet of wall in a day—a pro might do ten—and come sundown, you're more than ready for a rest. It can also be expensive. If you have to buy the stone, expect to pay between $250 to $300 a ton, keeping in mind that a four-foot (1.2-m) section of wall easily eats up a ton of stone. Fortunately, you might be able to come by sufficient stone for next to nothing—indeed, the stone used to make the wall pictured in this story was harvested from a farmer's field.

A skilled mason can build a dry stone wall that stands eight feet high (more than 2 m), as well as arches and bridges, but novices are more likely to start with something simpler. Even a three-foot wall, like the one shown here built by me (pictured in green shirt) and a colleague named Dean McLellan (in plaid shirt, right), has tons of charm. There's nothing stopping you. Leave no stone unturned.

Tools & Equipment Required

WHEELBARROW to deliver the stones to the work site

BUCKET for small stones, especially hearting

STRING LINES AND FRAME to set the shape and batter (see Step 2) of the wall

HAMMER for breaking large stones into hearting (see Step 3); for knocking off a chunk to make a stone fit better

RUBBERIZED GLOVES work better than leather for handling tons of wet muddy stone; your hands will thank you

PILLOW your knees will thank you

Step by step

THE WALL shown here is a little over three feet high. At the base it is two feet wide, tapering to a width of one foot at the top.

STEP 1
Getting Ready

Mark the extent of the wall with a string line. (Use a garden hose if the wall is to have a curve.) Ideally, it should measure 26 inches (65 cm) wide. Excavate the soil to a depth of about 6 inches (15 cm) (a). To ensure good drainage, fill with ¾-inch crushed gravel (b). This marks the footprint of the wall.

It doesn't sound like much of a foundation, but some masons don't even go this far and build the wall directly on the ground. Despite its enormous weight, nothing fancier is required; frost action should not be a problem because the stones—without mortar—are free to give and take with the seasons.

Gather enough stones to lay about 10 feet (3 m) of wall and dump them randomly where they will be handy for inspection as you work. For ease of movement, leave a 2-foot (60-cm) path between the wall and the pile of rocks.

STEP 2
Setting the Batter

For structural strength, a dry stone wall must have a "batter," that is, an incline so that the base of the wall (c) is wider than the crown (d). Batter is crucial to structural integrity, so that frost action will pitch the stones inward on themselves, while gravity holds the wall intact. Without it, gravity and frost would soon heave the stones outward and break the wall into fragments. The batter of the wall should lean in approximately two inches (5 cm) for every vertical foot (30 cm).

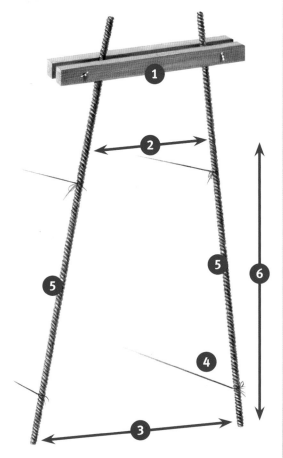

1 Wooden spacers held together with bolts and wing nuts

2 Width at top (W1)

3 Width at base (W2), 28″ (70 cm) to 36″ (90 cm)

4 String line

5 Rebar (hammered into ground)

6 Height (H) of wall (less coping) equals width of base + width at top; $H = W1 + W2$

STEP 2 CONT'D.

Batter can be less if the stones are uniformly flat.

Rare is the mason who can eyeball proper batter. Even the pros use some kind of form to keep the incline consistent. Using rebars and wood, we rigged two frames (see illustration at left), one placed at each end of the excavation. String lines run from the corners of one frame to the corresponding corners of the other, acting as a guide for placement of the top course. This ensures the batter is regular.

STEP 3
Choosing the Stones

Note that almost every stone has a "good side" or "face" (e) that is relatively smooth and regular. As construction progresses, be sure to lay each stone with the face on view. Although it's tempting to expose the long dimension, the face is almost always on the short end—this is for structural reasons, so that the length of the stone is knit into the guts of the wall. If a stone is so shapeless that it doesn't have a face, it can still be used for "hearting," that

is, fill for the interior of the wall. Meanwhile, save stones with two faces for the corners (Step 5). Keep the flattest for the coping (see Step 7).

STEP 4
Base Course

Lay the first course, reserving the largest, heaviest and most irregular boulders for the base (f). Fill the voids in between with smaller stones. Do the entire length of the wall, including hearting, before attempting the second course.

STEP 5
Corners

The ends rise first (g). They are more complicated than the rest of the wall as the corners ought to be dove-tailed to ensure structural rigidity. Even so, the basic rules of masonry still apply—see Step 6.

STEP 6
Laying the Courses

Place each stone with the short face on view (h). For good drainage and structure, the stones shouldn't lie exactly flat, but tilt outward toward the edges of the wall a little. To get the right incline, wedge smaller stones under larger ones (i). Fill the gaps and the interior with hearting. Working as a team—one person on one side, the partner on the other—build the wall, course by course, in four-foot sections (j).

Secrets of a Stone Mason

• Any kind of stone—from round boulders to flat river stones—can be used for a dry stone wall, but flat stones tend to be easier to work with.

• Don't rush the work.

• Place a stone, and then build around it. It's easier than looking for the right stone for a specific spot.

• Each stone should touch as many others as possible.

• The bulk of a stone should not be on view. Most of it should be knitted into the interior of the wall.

k

STEP 6 CONT'D.

There's an old adage in mason's circles that goes, "One stone over two, two stones over one." Keep this in mind as you lay each course; if you follow this basic rule, you will ensure that there won't be any vertical seams between courses. Much the way a brick wall is stronger if the joints are staggered, this greatly improves the integrity of the structure.

From time to time, stand back and admire your work. Check for flaws in the structure and alignment, and sight along the string line (k) to see that the batter is maintained. If you spot a flaw, don't sweat it—it's easy to tear down a section and start over. (You can't say that about concrete!)

As you progress, you'll develop an eye for the craft. Although never as precise as a mortar wall, the courses should be fairly even and follow a uniform, horizontal pattern (l). Never lay a stone in an upright position (m). Occasionally, you'll find a stone that is large enough to be

a "through stone" (n), which can straddle the entire width of the work—these are a nice touch, but by no means necessary. Another mark of a skilled mason is to incorporate round boulders into the wall (o). So are serpentine curves, but these may be beyond the reach of a first-time builder. Even so, there's no doubt that you'll graduate from greenhorn to artist before you finish—you'll see the wall as a unit, not just a pile of rocks.

STEP 7
Finishing Touches

The conventional finish is to cap the wall with a coping row—flat stones arranged like books on a shelf. With a slight lean, coping looks to the uninitiated like it could be easily toppled over, but just try it. Each stone leans into the next, keeping the row surprisingly tight.

An alternative to coping is a turf top (see picture on page 200), which sprouts grass. It starts with a layer of impervious landscape matting laid atop the top row of stone. Next, a layer of sod is applied, green side down, over which a second layer of sod is laid, green side up. If kept sufficiently watered, the grass should thrive, as the lower layer of sod provides enough soil while the matting prevents it from drying out.

Country Careers

by Bridget Wayland

Tired of the long commute to work? Finding it hard to get your job done in the midst of chatty co-workers, constant interruptions or long, fruitless meetings? Sick of having your supervisor take credit for your good work? Maybe it's time to make a break for it.

Thanks to the phone, the fax and the Internet, you don't have to be in a conventional office to get your job done. Nor do you have to live in the city. As the information highway pushes its way into rural environs, a whole new range of opportunities is emerging for people who want to work at home…and live in the country.

Pursuing a career in the country must suit a low-stress country lifestyle and reflect personal interests.

We're not just talking Mary Kay and real estate franchises, here. From niche-market farming to running your own bed and breakfast, working from home allows you to tailor your job to your own rhythm. You can dress the way you want, set your own hours, and focus entirely on the task at hand in the undisturbed oasis of your home office.

Of course, working from home has a special appeal when you live in the country. By discontinuing your daily drive to work, you can devote that commuting time to something that brings you personal satisfaction. Why not take a long walk with the dogs every day, or devote that extra hour to stacking firewood or kneading bread?

Working at home is economical, too. Not only do you save on horrendous gas costs, but you can also greatly reduce your budget for clothing and overpriced lunches. What's more, if you're going to be working from home, you'll have extra time and money to invest in livestock or vegetable farming—a sideline in beef cattle, chickens, berries or asparagus may suddenly become an option.

Even better, working from home a few days a week takes the pressure off daycare expenses for young parents, and allows them to spend more time with their kids. But best of all, when you work at home, your time is your own. As long as you get the work done, you can take breaks as needed to tend to your household, crop and animal needs, all the while earning a significant outside income.

Today's home-based businesses run the gamut from mushroom farming to webmastering (maintaining a client's website). But to make the cut, the following list of *Harrowsmith Country Life*'s ten best home-based careers had to meet a few criteria. They must be able to provide a decent living, demand reasonably low start-up costs, require no extra employees, offer sufficient time off to pursue personal interests, and suit a low-stress country lifestyle. Naturally, there are many other home-business opportunities, but these are ten of our favourites, in no particular order.

Bed & Breakfast

DO TOURISTS FLOCK to your neck of the woods? Do you have a beautiful, spacious home? And more importantly, do you love to entertain? If you answered yes to all three, perhaps it's your calling to open a bed and breakfast. B & B is great for empty nesters who don't need much privacy, and for those who are happy staying home every weekend. With a good occupancy rate and five guest rooms, you can make a decent living at it, although the going can be tough for anyone with a hefty mortgage. Much depends on the amount of business and tourist traffic through your burg, not to mention your ability to attract repeat business.

Niche Market Farming

WE'VE SAID IT before and we'll say it again. One of the few remaining arenas in which the small-scale farm can still turn a decent profit is the production of gourmet food products for speciality markets. Growing organic garlic or salad greens, for instance, requires lots of hands-on labour and copious fertilizer such as manure and compost, but only a small land base. What's more, it offers a significantly larger return per acre than large-scale crop farming operations, and with the right marketing skills, is eminently suited to a home-based business. Other niche products include cut flowers, sprouts, mushrooms and herbs, as well as various value-added products such as pickles, preserves and herbal teas.

Installing Solar Panels

ONE OF THE best things about living in the country is that you can tap into cheaper, more environmentally friendly forms of energy and thus gain partial, or even total independence from the big utility companies. There are several forms of renewable energy, including geothermal, wind, hydro and solar, all of which are gaining in popularity. To make money as an alternative energy equipment installer, however, solar panels are often considered the best bet. With special training and the know-how to sell and install solar heating systems, you'll find clients in environmentally conscious homeowners, hotels located far off the beaten track, and work-at-home entrepreneurs who need reliable computer and Internet access, even when the power goes off.

Selling Country Crafts on the Web

WHETHER YOU MAKE grapevine baskets, twig furniture, or beeswax candles, you can turn your favourite hobby into a profitable, home-based business by marketing your wares in today's Yellow Pages—the Internet. Artisan crafts have a widespread appeal that need not be confined to the limits of your local market. As long as you have sufficient raw materials, work space and time available to produce products in mass quantities, you can use a website to reach a much wider audience. Include your telephone number so that customers can place their orders in the traditional way, or if you prefer, provide your site with a secure credit card shopping capability. The time required to monitor your website, transactions and shipping can be significant, but then, so can the financial rewards.

Home Care Services

WITH THE FIRST wave of baby boomers just reaching their golden years, the demand for home care is shooting through the roof. Home care is a range of medical and domestic services that allows aging and ill Canadians to remain at home in safety and dignity for as long as possible. Private home care workers run the gamut from nurses, social workers, nutritionists and dietitians to therapists—occupational, speech, respiratory and physio, but you can also tap into the market through home support (homemaking, personal care, meal services, minor home repair and maintenance) or social contact services (friendly visiting, telephone reassurance). By providing a daily checkup for homebound patients, assisting them with daily hygiene and nutrition, and even performing light housekeeping duties, you will be a godsend to the more than 2.8 million family caregivers in Canada, who will gladly pay for private services to ensure quality care for their loved ones.

Restoring Homes and Furnishings

THE SUCCESSIVE WAVES of urban refugees who buy old properties in the countryside are a ripe market for a local contractor who specializes in restoring old homes and antique furnishings. Whether you can strip and refinish furniture, refurbish enamelled iron bathroom fixtures, sand and stain pine floors to their original sheen, or even restore a fieldstone foundation, you could create a lucrative, full-time home business for yourself. You'll need a special skill, the proper equipment, and the know-how to reach and satisfy your clients. Of course, it helps to have a good understanding of historic building and furniture styles. Don't overlook local commercial clients, for whom the "ye olde country store" look may be worth its weight in gold.

Writing Services

THANKS TO FAX machines, email and the Internet, the well-connected freelance writer can easily work from a country home. If writing, editing, proofreading, or translation is your bag, there's nothing stopping you from doing this work from home, where you can watch the deer feed in the meadow while you sit at your computer writing brochure copy. Make sure you get into the city on a regular basis, however, because networking is the best way to reach new clients, and person-to-person contact is crucial if you want to keep the core clientele you already have. These days, the most profitable fields for professional writers are technical writing (product manuals and instructional materials), copywriting (advertisements, sales brochures and other promotional materials), and corporate communications (press kits, speeches, reports, newsletters). Desktop publishing, where you edit, design and lay out these printed materials, is also a hot home-business idea.

Computer and Web Services

Almost everyone has a personal computer these days. But for every Joe or Jill who knows how to debug the thing, there are a dozen Luddites who cannot cope with the slightest computer glitch. And without a friendly neighbourhood computer guru to come in and set things straight, these data-munching triumphs of modern technology often become used as expensive dust magnets in bedrooms across the countryside. If you have the know-how to repair computers, or better yet, provide tutorial services to clueless baby boomers who got a PC for Christmas, you could conceivably quit your day job tomorrow morning. Other hot computer-related home businesses include freelance programming (systems and/or applications), creating websites for local businesses and maintaining sites as a webmaster.

Business Support Services

In this era of corporate downsizing, more and more companies are outsourcing administrative work and office support services on a project-by-project basis. If you are a whiz with word processing, database management and email communication, have impeccable organizational skills and considerable secretarial experience and the contacts to match, you can serve a network of clients from your own home. Of course, spreadsheets and business letters are only one possible focus. Staff-strapped offices also outsource bookkeeping, billing, Internet research and so on. Whatever your business specialty, you can sell it to companies far and wide, and you don't have to leave your home office to do it.

Cleaning Services

Cleaning services are perhaps the easiest business to launch. Of course, it's not for everyone—the first rule of starting your own home-based business is to do what you love. If you are the kind of person who enjoys the satisfaction of a mess well cleaned, there is a strong market for your services. Families where both parents work outside the home often don't have the time for proper housecleaning, but will gladly pay someone to come in on an occasional or routine basis. While kitchens, floors and windows may be the mainstay of the industry, there are also successful cleaning businesses that specialize in chimneys, ceilings, carpets, cars, pools, and innumerable other niches.

Five Sure-Fire Tips for Success

1. Manage Your Time

Without a supervisor keeping them on their toes, home-based workers have to be good at managing their time. Without the requisite discipline, it's easy to let a home business eat up your evenings and weekends unnecessarily. Conversely, it can also be hard to get the job done when there's laundry to do, snow to shovel, the TV to watch, and hometown buddies only a phone call away. Set your office hours, and stick to them.

2. Stay in Touch

There is some truth to the old maxim "Out of sight, out of mind." Counter this tendency by taking the initiative to stay in touch with your old colleagues.

Prevent isolation by keeping up with the business community at large—try joining the local chamber of commerce, as well as a relevant professional or trade association. Likewise, while the Internet, fax and email make it possible to do most of your work at home, take every opportunity to meet face-to-face, particularly with new clients.

3. Maintain Professionalism

While a creativity-stifling office atmosphere may be precisely what you want to get away from, maintaining a professional attitude at home is just as important. After all, the cleanliness and professionalism of your work space set the tone for clients entering your home office.

Even if you're the only person to set foot in the office, good organization is the key to maintaining that professional edge. Likewise, you might consider installing a separate business phone line, especially if you have kids—nothing spells risk to a potential client quite like their call being answered by a surly teen.

4. Do Your Homework

Before you take the plunge, learn as much as possible about marketing strategies and efficient office management skills. At the very least, you'll need to identify your ideal customers, ferret out their needs, and choose the most effective marketing methods to reach them. Developing a good business plan is another key to success. You might also investigate what's involved in setting up and maintaining a website, with or without the capacity for e-commerce. After all, it's your future at stake.

5. Get Help

You may have been outstanding at your old job, whether that was installing solar panels for an electrical company or translating government documents, but when you strike out on your own, your job description balloons far beyond your particular area of expertise. Without the support of a secretarial staff, marketing and sales team, office manager, graphic designer and bookkeeper, some home entrepreneurs may feel lost.

The answer? Hire the services of an accountant, financial planner, lawyer and other consultants as needed, and contract out some skilled tasks such as tabulating data or editing your sales materials. It may increase your overhead, but consider it a crucial business investment.

Vegetables by Design

by Bridget Wayland

ARE VEGETABLE GARDENS beautiful? Many of us still consider them drab, utilitarian spaces best relegated to an out-of-the-way part of the backyard, even though we spend more time laying them out and tending them than we do our perennial border. Perhaps it's time to blur the distinction between the "practical" vegetable patch and the "attractive" flower bed.

After all, we grow vegetables for pleasure, too. Who hasn't paused in their weeding to admire neat green rows of carrots in the freshly turned soil, or taken a moment to savour the incredible scent while pinching out tomato suckers? There's an incredible range of colour and form in those productive plants, many of which have delicate flowers just as beautiful as any sweet pea.

The following three design options recognize the vegetable garden for what it is: a bold, intricate and, yes, beautiful creation deserving of a more prominent place in the home landscape.

Interplanting vegetables with flowers benefits their health. For instance, nicotiana is said to repel potato beetles, French marigolds to fight nematodes, and nasturtiums to ward off aphids.

Option One

Beauty in Symmetry

AT ONE EXTREME is a highly organized, formal plan known as the "four-square." It works best on a small scale, 18 by 20 feet (5 m by 6 m). This is the traditional kitchen garden design used in medieval monasteries and was transplanted to North America by colonial settlers.

Two main paths, one vertical and one horizontal, cross in the middle of the garden, dividing the whole space into quadrants. Each quadrant is the mirror image of the others. This symmetrical design is anchored into place by a framework of permanent raised beds made of 2 x 8 cedar planks.

In the past, these gardens were built around a source of water at the very centre. Today, a birdbath, statuary, bench, scarecrow or other garden ornament could also serve as a focal point. If you prefer, just use it as an uncluttered turning circle for your wheelbarrow.

A four-square garden is usually enclosed. Walls create a sheltered microclimate, provide structure for vertical gardening and help keep out pests (traditionally, roaming livestock and neighbourhood rogues; today more likely deer and dogs). Any kind of fencing will do, although a cedar split-rail or picket fence provides a relaxed, cottage garden ambience.

If you like, you can emphasize the formal nature of the four-square design by combining plants for aesthetic effect. Experiment with simple geometric patterns, using plants of different colours and shapes. Each bed can display its own personality while contributing to the overall design. The result shouldn't look like a stuffy municipal planting, but rather like a charming patchwork quilt.

Don't get bogged down in positioning plants for aesthetic effect. These concerns are important only insofar as they support good horticultural practices, such as proper spacing, maximizing sun exposure, compatible plant pairings and succession planting.

Obviously, this formal design takes careful planning. It can be difficult to fit all your veggies into beds of fixed, irregular dimensions. Thankfully, you only have to get out your graph paper once. After you've devised a plan that works, you can stick with it year after year. To rotate your crops, you just plant the same things in the quadrant next door.

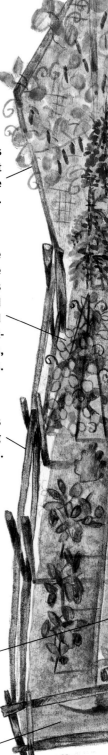

An eight-foot-tall (2.5-m) trellis attached to the fence makes it possible to save garden space by training vines vertically.

Tucked up against the fence at the northern side of the garden, these beds enjoy a warm, sheltered microclimate. They're filled with a single row of heat-lovers: cherry tomatoes, basil and cayenne peppers.

A cedar split-rail fence defines the space without blocking sunlight or air circulation.

This bed has onion sets planted in the outline of a diamond, with carrots in the middle and beets and radishes all around.

A low hedge of parsley, basil, nasturtiums or marigolds serves as edible edging.

Option One: The Four-Square Garden

A central bench provides a great resting place from which to admire the garden.

Permanent raised beds, eight inches high (20 cm), provide better drainage and easier care.

A bed of blade-shaped leeks is interplanted with feathery dill for an interesting contrast in form, if not colour.

This rectangular bed is divided diagonally for aesthetic effect, with kale on one side and Brussels sprouts on the other.

The main entrance is framed by a cedar arbour draped with snow peas and scarlet runner beans.

Zucchini sprawls out of its confines and into the path, nicely blurring the formality of the design.

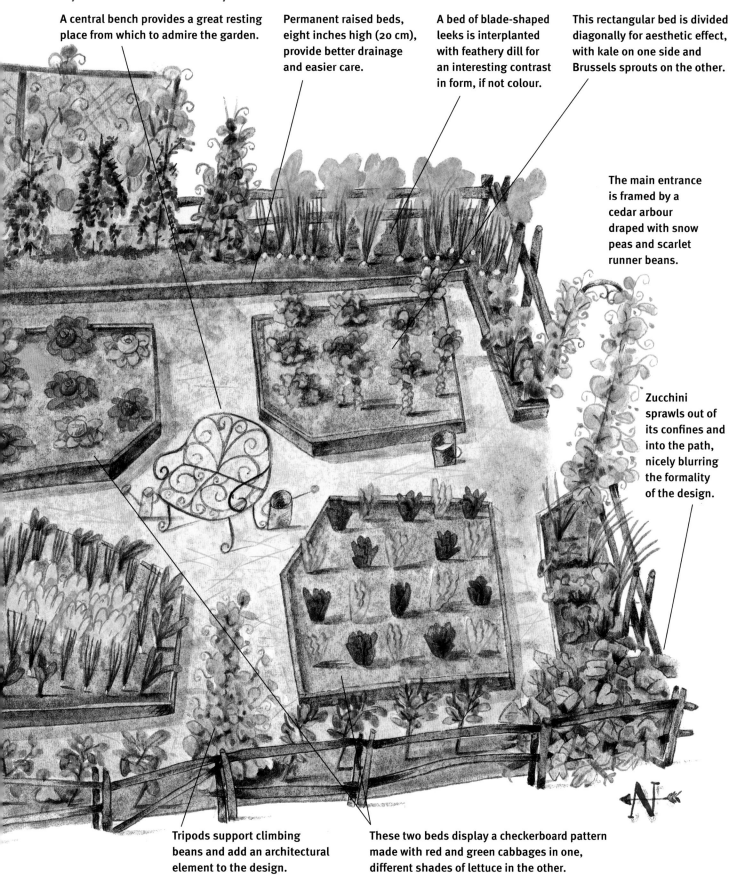

Tripods support climbing beans and add an architectural element to the design.

These two beds display a checkerboard pattern made with red and green cabbages in one, different shades of lettuce in the other.

Option Two

Beauty in Simplicity

OUR SECOND garden design—"cornrows"—is perhaps the most familiar, especially for old-school back-to-the-landers. It's basically a large rototilled area that's planted in long, thin rows, like a field of corn. At 30 by 60 feet (9 m by 18 m), this type of garden tends to be big, maybe too big.

The advantage of this approach is that the whole thing can be designed on the fly, and there's virtually no paperwork, save a few words scrawled in a notebook: the number of feet planted; the variety name; the date. In terms of advance planning, you merely have to calculate how many "feet of row" will be needed for each vegetable to produce the desired yield at harvest time. You go out and plant your seeds in a straight line, and when you've reached the other side of the garden, you just skip over a few feet and start a new row. When you've sown enough of one thing, you put in a stake and move on to the next. Simple.

Like anything, though, this type of garden design does have its drawbacks. For instance, leaving a wide path between every two rows does make it easy to access all the plants, but then again, it's not really good for them to have their root zone compacted from foot traffic on all sides.

Weeding is another issue. Long, straight rows are a cinch to weed, as you can scrape a hoe blade down either side of the line without danger of seedling decapitation. Good thing, too, because this design leaves a great deal of garden soil unplanted, churned up and exposed to sunlight—perfect conditions for sprouting dormant weed seeds. Be prepared to do a lot of weeding, or spread a lot of mulch.

What's more, planting in thin rows is almost silly from an efficiency standpoint, since it wastes so much space on pathways. Even if you reduce each path to a minimum width of 18″ (45 cm), you're still devoting half the total area of your garden to non-productive use. This means your garden has to be bigger to fit in everything you want to grow. The larger the area, the more work for you, and the less return (harvest) for your labour.

Nevertheless, this design offers one big benefit: No matter how you plant your garden, the slate can be wiped clean at the end of each season with a few passes of the rototiller. If you want to plant half the space in pumpkins one year, you can. Anything is possible.

Staked tomatoes take up a lot of space, but provide an excellent harvest.

Early and late beans are planted amidst this row of tomatoes.

Zucchini sprawls out at the far end of the garden.

All the roots are grouped together: a couple of rows of onions, carrots and beets grow right next to the potato patch.

Option Two: The Cornrow Garden

Rows run north–south, so all plants get their fair share of direct sunlight.

Early peas climb a trellis erected at the outside edge of the garden.

Perennial crops, such as chives, rhubarb, sage, asparagus and strawberries, are grouped together at one side, out of the tiller's way.

This row is reserved for early spring plantings. When the plants go to seed, rip them out and replant a second crop in the same place.

Plant herbs by the garden's main entrance for convenient dinnertime snipping.

To save space, alternate rows of early-maturing crops with rows of late-season space-hogs. Here, winter squash vines stretch into a long-vacated row of lettuce.

Peppers, broccoli, Brussels sprouts and eggplants all take approximately the same amount of space in this long row.

A short row of lettuce is snuck in between winter squash and Brussels sprouts.

Corn is planted in a block of short rows for good pollination.

Option Three

Beauty in Efficiency

Winter squash flow into cornrows and pathways. Mulch well in June.

Two blocks of sweet corn, running NW–SE for sun exposure.

Seedbed for perennial flowers such as echinacea and columbine.

Crops that need frequent picking, such as lettuce, herbs, snap beans and summer squash, are planted on either side of main path for easy access.

T HIS DESIGN COMBINES the best of both worlds. It's flexible like the cornrows garden, but attractive like the four-square. As an informal garden planted in temporary wide rows, it's more efficient in its use of space than either.

This is the type of plan we use for the *Harrowsmith Country Life* trial garden. At 30 by 60 feet (9 m by 18 m), it is large enough to grow ten varieties of everything, including space-hungry crops such as corn, potatoes or pumpkins, but this design works well on a small scale too. However, no matter how big the garden, it's always a challenge to squeeze everything in.

This garden is designed to minimize pathways by using densely planted wide beds as its basic building block. Their configuration changes a little every year, but the beds are generally about four feet (1.2 m) wide and four inches (10 cm) high. They're laid out parallel to one another across the slope of the garden, like subtle terraces, to trap rainwater and prevent soil erosion.

The path to the main entrance is wide enough for a wheelbarrow to pass, but the other paths are kept to two feet (0.6 m) or so—just wide enough for weeding, staking, pruning and harvesting the plants easily from both sides of the bed. Many of the paths terminate in blind alleys at the far side of the garden, to maximize the available planting space.

The beds themselves are intensively planted, leaving no unnecessary gaps in which weeds can sprout and moisture can evaporate. Any holes are filled by popping in a nasturtium seed or a clump of herbs.

In fact, this garden is rife with blossoms. Interplanting vegetables with flowers not only accentuates their natural beauty but also benefits their health, since bright colours and strong perfumes may help attract good bugs and repel bad. For instance, nicotiana is said to repel potato beetles, French marigolds to fight nematodes, and nasturtiums to ward off aphids.

And that's not all the blooms are good for. Edible flowers like borage and calendula grow among the lettuce patches to add colour to the salad bowl. Other annuals, such as cosmos, California poppies, sunflowers and zinnias, also have a useful place in the garden, as they can't help but cheer us up while we work.

The end result? A tight, efficiently planned garden that looks good enough to eat.

Option Three: The Informal Garden

Two staggered rows of eggplants and peppers, interplanted with nasturtiums.

Five hills of watermelon on black plastic in hottest part of garden.

Ten rows of bush snap beans with a band of marigolds on far side.

Four hills of summer squash (zucchini, scallop, crookneck, eight-ball).

Three hills of cucumbers spread out beneath tomatoes.

Undisturbed corner for rhubarb, perennial herbs such as chives, lemon balm and sage. We added spring bulbs and Madonna lilies, for the pleasure of gazing at them as we prepared the garden in springtime.

Row of giant sunflowers along the top (northwest side) where they won't shade everything else. For fun, plant gladioli at their feet.

A border of tough perennials, such as phlox and daylilies, runs down the side closest to the house.

30 tomato plants on tripods interplanted with carrots and beets.

Ten rows of heirloom shelling beans climb sturdy cedar poles.

Early peas climb a tall trellis about 10 feet (3 m) long. Bed is filled with bush peas on one side, spinach on the other. Planted in April, replaced with lima beans in June.

Potatoes interplanted with a row of garlic, nicotiana and marigolds. Early varieties are grouped together.

Do It Yourself

Bubbling with ideas for this year's vegetable garden? Here's how to get your design started.

Tomatoes

SPACING: 2 feet (60 cm) apart, staked. Rows 3 feet (90 cm) apart

YIELD: 6 to 24 fruits per plant

NEED: 6 slicing and 14 paste tomatoes. Total 20 plants.

AREA: 40 by 2 feet (12 m by 60 cm)

First, make a list of everything you want to grow. Consult a good gardening book and jot down the proper spacing and expected yield for each of these vegetables (see example above).

Next, estimate how much produce your household can handle, and determine how many plants you will need for such a harvest.

Finally, crunch these figures to see how much area each crop will require in the garden.

Will you have enough room for everything? Go out and measure your garden (each stride equals about three feet (1 m), more or less). Translate its proportions to graph paper, using one square for each foot (or any convenient metric equivalent).

On your diagram, split up the garden into parallel bands, six feet (1.8 m) wide, running north-south (or across the slope if your garden is on an incline). Split each of these bands into two strips: a planting bed four feet wide (1.2 m), and below it, a path two feet (60 cm) wide (see Fig. 1). If some fiddling is necessary, widen the central pathway. Remember, you don't need paths along the edges.

This sketch represents the bare bones of your garden. Flesh them out by adding vegetables, one crop at a time. Carrots, beets, lettuce and other small plants are easy to slot in, so start with veggies that need more space. For instance, each hill of winter squash will eat up an area six feet (1.8 m) in diameter, and it's useless to grow corn in blocks less than six feet (1.8 m) square.

Draw circles to represent the eventual spread of each plant (or block of small plants), with a dot in the middle showing where to plant them. Try to arrange the circles so they cover the entire bed, leaving no gaps for the sun to beam through. The trick to creating this solid canopy of leaves is to stagger your plants in a triangular pattern, rather than planting in a grid (see Fig 2).

For example, you would position the first two tomato seedlings across one end of a bed, 12 inches (30 cm) from the edge, 24 inches (60 cm) apart. Plant the third seedling in the centre of the bed, 24 inches (60 cm) from the first two, forming a triangle. Start the pattern again with two more seedlings planted abreast, 24 inches (60 cm) diagonally from the third. And so on, all the way down the bed.

This kind of intensive planting scheme allows you to fit more into a smaller space. For instance, those 20 tomato plants will fit comfortably in an area 23 feet long and four feet wide (7 m by 1.2 m), without the need to waste space on a path between them. There is even

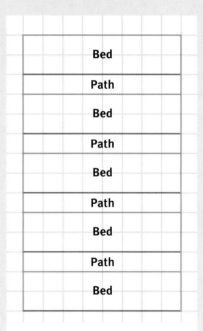

Fig. 1 1 sq = 2 feet (60 cm)
Sketch the bare bones of your garden before you pencil in the crops. Here, reddish lines split the diagram into six-foot (2 m) bands; green lines mark out wide beds and narrow paths.

room to sow a crop of late lettuce in the shady nooks on either side of the single plants.

Here are a few more design principles to consider when positioning your plants into the wide-bed design.

• Avoid planting a large block of any bug-prone crop. Instead, disperse the plants in several small patches. By the same logic, don't concentrate all the plants from a given family in the same area of the garden—cucumber bugs will be delighted to discover your squash and melons, for instance.

• Sort your wish list by harvest date (early, mid-summer, fall), and pair up vegetables that can occupy the same bed at different times. For instance, you could plant spinach, peas, leaf lettuce and carrots in the tomato bed almost two months before transplant time. These early crops will be harvested long before the tomatoes need the space.

• Jot down which plants make good companions for each of your crops, and make space for them in your plan. This is a great way to start incorporating flowers and herbs into the garden.

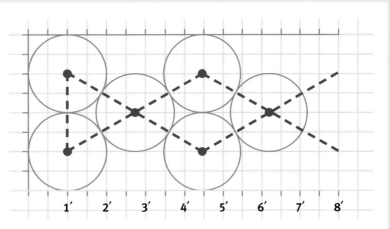

Fig. 2 1 sq = 6 inches (15 cm)
Triangular spacing in a four-foot-wide (1.2 m) bed, showing the eventual spread of staked tomato plants. Space each pair 3½ feet (1 m) apart, and then pop one more into the middle. Can fill the gaps with late lettuce.

• Note the height of each variety, and strive to keep tall things to the north of short things, unless you want to shade them.

• Figure out which of your crops should and should not succeed each other, and you can develop your own personal crop rotation scheme. In general, you don't want to plant something in the same place two years in a row, or even follow it with a related plant. This discourages soil-borne diseases, prevents insect populations from building up, and prevents nutrient depletion.

• Once you've created a design, don't be afraid to vary it. Try different combinations of plants and experiment with unfamiliar varieties—there are more out there than you could grow in a lifetime.

With all these factors to consider, creating a great design can be a tricky process. But above all, it should be fun: a perfect fusion of practicality and pleasure.

Heirlooms in the Barnyard

A *Harrowsmith Country Life* Staff Report

AT FIRST, IT sounds like an exercise in pure nostalgia. Tom Hutchinson, professor of ecology and agriculture at Trent University by day and hobby farmer in his off-hours, raises Cotswold sheep at his farm near Indian River, Ontario. Descendants of a line that originated in the hills and dales of northern England, the Cotswold sheep was once common on Canadian farms and prized in Grandfather's day as the backbone of the woollen industry. But through most of the 20th century, it was a dying breed, a victim of the move to synthetic fibres. That is, until Tom and like-minded farmers made a conscious effort to reverse the trend. "Only a few years ago, there were a mere 38 animals left in Canada," he says with some urgency in his voice. "We couldn't let them die off—such a fine old breed deserves better."

Pity the poor Sebastopol goose, whose numbers are in serious decline. Sadly, it's not the only farm animal whose future is uncertain.

The Canadienne, noted among other things for its amenable temperament and the rich milk it produces, is the oldest breed of cattle in North America.

By actively recruiting farmers to devote time and space to the breed, Cotswold numbers have bounced back from the brink. They are still a rare sight, but with a current population of over 300, their chances seem better.

But there's more behind Tom's efforts than sentiment. He and his colleagues at Rare Breeds Canada, a non-profit group dedicated to preserving the bloodlines of any number of nearly extinct barnyard animals, have a more serious mission in mind. "Modern agriculture is on a dangerous course," he warns. With so much of agri-business dedicated to the bottom line, there has been a major push toward standardization of livestock: Only the breeds that perform best—the chickens that lay the most eggs, the cows that produce the most milk, the turkeys that fatten up the fastest—have a place in modern farming. "When one breed is favoured over all others, you get a monoculture, which is very unhealthy in the long run," he says.

All it takes is a drive through dairy country and you can see what Tom means. Where once you might have seen Jerseys and Guernseys, Ayrshires and maybe even the odd Canadienne, today's dairy farms are a patchwork of black and white. Years ago, the Holstein won the crown as the breed of choice for its ability to produce buckets and buckets of milk. Indeed, today it alone accounts for 90 percent of all dairy cows in Canada. But did you know that, thanks to the universal adoption of artificial insemination, almost half the current Canadian herd was sired by a mere 11 bulls? This has Tom Hutchinson worried, for recently, one of these bulls was discovered to carry a genetic defect—which may have long-term consequences for its legions of descendants. Its female offspring are prone to stillbirths and miscarriages.

"What happens if inbreeding spoils the Holstein?" Tom asks rhetorically. "With so much of the dairy industry reliant on one cow, are there enough other breeds to pick up the slack in case of an emergency?" For that reason alone, it's easy to see why the work of Rare Breeds Canada goes beyond mere nostalgia.

Past and present, there have been cracks in the genetics of other prized barnyard animals, too. For example, the Yorkshire pig was so good at making bacon that it accounted for 90 percent of the hog population by the 1940s. Trouble was, it was prone to serious respiratory problems. Today's meat chickens are susceptible to heart attack, thanks to the extra strain of carrying around so much breast meat. And while Leghorn-hybrid layers can produce vast quantities of eggs, they have largely lost their mothering instincts—heaven help them if they ever had to raise a family.

In light of this, Rare Breeds Canada sees its work as part of an even bigger picture. How will mainstream farm animals fare in the future, it asks, in a world of climate change and uncertainty over resources? Indeed, the prospects look dim for many of today's popular breeds, which wouldn't survive long without the benefits of an artificial, technology-dependent environment. "They don't stand much of a chance against global warming, drought, famine, El Niños and extreme winters," Tom suggests "However, heritage breeds might easily come to the rescue, since many of them were bred to withstand extreme conditions and disease in the first place." But although the cause has far-reaching implications, never doubt that at the heart of the preservation movement is a reverence for history and cheering for the underdog.

Margot Morris raises Sebastopol geese in rural New Brunswick.

A Gaggle of Sebastopol Geese

THE STATE OF the domestic goose is typical of what might be called the one-breed-fits-all syndrome. A single breed—the Embden—so dominates the scene that others are quickly falling by the wayside. It doesn't help that geese are no longer a routine presence on the country homestead: Alas, as the family farm continues to decline, so goes the goose population.

Geese serve several purposes: they put meat on the table; provide the occasional egg; they keep bugs down; and they're better than watchdogs when intruders come calling. And they provide feathers. "That's where the Sebastopol goose excels," says Margot Morris, who included this rare eastern European breed in her collection of 115 waterfowl on her 100-acre farm near Moncton, New Brunswick. Indeed, their plumage is unique: visibly curly and incredibly dense. "The curly feathers are the absolute best for stuffing pillows, quilted linings and other uses. That's why they were bred." Sebastopols hail from eastern Europe, where they are known as the Danube, Frizzle or Locken. They have been seen in grey and saddleback, but the standard in North America is white with an orange beak, sort of a long-haired version of the ubiquitous Embden. Never raised in large numbers in the first place, the Sebastopol is positively hurting now, The breed is only about 700 strong in Canada, and Margot is one of just a handful of breeders on this side of the Atlantic. "It's frustrating, because customs and livestock regulations make importing stock from Europe prohibitive."

While Sebastopols are her sentimental favourite, Margot understands their shortcomings. "They make good parents, but can't be relied on to reproduce viable eggs each year," she admits. And they're expensive—today, they are considered show birds and at $150 a pop, they cost about three times as much as an

On her rural Ontario farmstead, Montana Jones has a soft spot for woolly Shropshire sheep.

Embden. Moreover, their greatest asset—their feathers—can be a drawback. "In full plumage, the feathers are so long that they trail on the ground, so it is an absolute necessity for them to have a large pond to swim in." For the mainstream farmer, these liabilities make Embdens look pretty good indeed, but for Margot, it's one more reason to persevere. "All the rare breeds have served us well and have asked for very little in return. I think we owe them."

A Rafter of Blue Slate Turkeys

THE SUPERMARKET TURKEY is a classic case of genetics gone awry. Farmed so intensely and bred with only the bottom line in mind, the turkey is a mere shadow of its ancestor, the agile wild North American turkey. Today, the average butterball hybrid, officially known as the broad-breasted white, can barely waddle because it is laden with so much breast meat. Indeed, the inflated breast leaves it prone to heart attack and worse, gets in the way of mating so that artificial insemination is the rule in the turkey barn. For hobby breeders, perhaps the worst thing is that the broad-breasted white is usually unfit for life on the farm. That's because the breed has adjusted to commercial conditions where they typically live in such cramped quarters with so many other birds that they have to be routinely inoculated and medicated just to survive. As a result, their immune systems have become so weak that they are not a good bet in anything but an artificial environment.

So what's a hobby turkey fancier to do? "Try heirloom stock," advises Bonnie Meikle who, with her husband Sheane is host to up to 400 vintage turkeys each year on her 20 acres near Ponoka, south of Edmonton. "The old types aren't so far removed from the wild. They can still breed naturally and best of all, their immune systems are healthy." Sadly, however, virtually all the hardy heritage birds are on the endangered list while the coddled broad-breasted white reigns.

Among Bonnie's favourite older varieties is the Blue Slate from the United States, so named for the blue tint to its feathers. "There isn't much difference between the various heritage birds," she says. "In fact, all turkeys, even the white, are considered the same breed, but there are certainly different types." Plumage is often the sole distinguishing factor. "Farmers bred for colour so that they could identify their own when the neighbourhood herded their birds together and drove them—on foot—to

Shropshire sheep were first recognized as a breed in 1859 by the Royal Agricultural Society.

market." No matter the colour, there is a big difference in taste. "The meat is firmer and, if the bird was allowed to range on grass, the flavour is gamier. By comparison, supermarket turkeys have the texture of marshmallows."

A Flock of Shropshire Sheep

IN ITS HEYDAY, the Shropshire from England was called the "rent-paying sheep." Like other dual-purpose breeds, it produced tasty meat and bushels of wool, but also had an edge, in that it routinely possessed many other characteristics not always found in a single breed. It was even-tempered and resistant to disease; it produced lambs that fattened up quickly and matured early. Best of all, the Shropshire was prolific—more often than not, a ewe would give birth to twins, which, to this day, is still a highly desirable trait in sheep. Moreover, ewes would still produce at age 12, no small feat compared to the average breed, which can stop lambing as early as seven.

Perhaps it's no wonder, then, that the Shropshire was an overnight sensation when first introduced. "Before World War I, almost one-third of the 20,000 registered sheep in Canada were Shrops," says enthusiast Montana Jones, who works as a writer and graphic designer when she isn't in the barn at her farm near Hastings, Ontario. When looking to try her hand at raising livestock, she had a natural affinity for Shropshires. "They're the quintessential sheep—woolly cap, dark face, black button eyes—the kind a kid in love with farm animals would picture."

Currently, Montana is host to 30 Shrops, which trace their ancestry to one of the last known purebred rams in Ontario. Hers is one of the larger flocks. "There were a mere 46 registrations in 2001 and only 24 in 2002," she states. "Their numbers are in drastic decline." Oddly enough, their undoing was one of the very traits that made them popular in the first place. Unlike most other breeds, Shropshires have woolly legs and faces—they were marketed under the slogan "Wool from the tip of the toes to the tip of the nose." Unfortunately, shearing a Shropshire is finicky work, especially around the eyes, and when time is money, sheep farmers prefer a breed that doesn't require so much effort. But Montana is optimistic, even though the population of the breed is only about 160 strong in Canada. "Shropshires still have an important place in agriculture: on homesteads, family farms and organic farms," she says. "It's a good sheep."

A Drove of Canadienne Cows

THE CANADIENNE IS the oldest breed of cattle in North America, and the only one to have been developed on this side of the pond—in Quebec. Derived from Bretonne and Normande cows brought over by the first French colonists, the bloodline was augmented by the very best beasts sent over by Louis XIV in the early 17th century. Not surprisingly, the Canadienne is known in Quebec as "the cow that founded the country."

Then, as now, the breed was valued for its hardy constitution, amenable temperament, ability to work the land, its meat, and very rich milk (4.25 percent butterfat, 3.6 percent protein). The Canadienne's milk production stays steady all year, but even so, its average yield is less than that of a Holstein. And therein lay its downfall.

As late as 1850, virtually all cattle in Quebec were Canadiennes. But by 1880, the figure had descended to 75 percent, as higher-yielding dairy breeds began replacing it. "We came close to losing the Canadienne when everyone switched to Holsteins," says farmer and educator Diane Beaulieu, "but now many of us are going back to the cow from our grandparents' day."

Diane and her husband, Jean-Noel Groleau, currently raise 20 purebred Canadiennes, including eight heifers, alongside 60

Canada's own cow, as shown by Diane Beaulieu, at her farm in the Eastern Townships.

Holsteins. Their 250-acre farm is in Compton, 20 minutes south of Sherbrooke in the heart of the Eastern Townships of Quebec. "In the 1820s, the Cochranes, parents of Senator-cum-Alberta cattle man Matthew Henry, kept 800 Rosedales here, a breed which became extinct a hundred years ago," says Diane. "I'm interested in the Canadienne because we work an ancestral farm where one breed has already been lost."

Should we ever come close to losing the breed again, Jean-Guy Bernier, secretary/manager of the Canadienne Cattle Breeders Association, is counting on gene banks. "Quebec has already banked 100 cryogenically frozen purebred Canadienne embryos," he reports.

Back on the farm, the Groleaus recently launched a pure Canadienne buttery, one of the best uses for the breed's steady supply of high-fat milk. "We're trying to interest people in the breed and inspire other farmers to do the same," says Diane.

Tapping Winter's Sweet Bounty

by Tom Cruickshank

IT'S A LONG story, but in the spring of 2003 I found myself in deepest, darkest Alabama, chatting to some born and bred southerners about the rituals of country living. They impressed me with tales of the pecan harvest—picking barrels of fresh nuts from the ground come September—which sounded positively exotic to a true Canuck like me. But that was nothing compared to their reaction when I fired back that I make my own maple syrup. As I explained the technique of tapping my trees, they hung on every word as if I was describing how I harvest coconuts on some faraway tropical isle. Indeed, maple syrup is a rare commodity south of the Mason-Dixon Line. "If you find it at all at the Piggly Wiggly," said one, almost drooling, "you'll pay at least 20 bucks for about a quarter of a pint."

From hearty country-style dishes to gourmet creations, chefs around the world have discovered the delicious, unmistakable flavour maple syrup adds to food.

237

It's easy for a Canadian, especially an easterner, to take maple syrup for granted. After all, it's on the shelves of every grocery store and as winter starts to wane each year, the sight of taps on trees is almost as common as wool on sheep. Sometimes we forget that maple syrup is renowned worldwide as a rare and delightful delicacy. Indeed, in Japan, they clamour for maple syrup the way wine connoisseurs look forward to Beaujolais nouveau. Gourmet chefs love maple's unmistakable flavour and have elevated it to exalted status in international cuisine. Here at home, maybe it's time that we gave the sweet nectar of the eastern forest its due. Like Anne of Green Gables, Mike Myers and the maple leaf itself, maple syrup is a national icon.

The origin of the maple syrup harvest is the stuff of lore, but it was well known to the First Nations, who showed the European settlers how to tap a certain deciduous tree—which became known, not surprisingly, as the sugar maple (*Acer saccharum*). It isn't the only hardwood tree that yields sweet sap, but it is by far the best. When boiled to just the right consistency and colour, the sap becomes a sweet elixir, much appreciated in an earlier era known for bland, subsistence diets and a dearth of conventional cane sugar. Although not necessarily a precise science, making syrup has never been for the fidgety—it takes about 40 gallons (152 litres) of sap to make one gallon (4 litres) of syrup—but patience is always well rewarded. Within a generation, "sugaring off" was an annual tradition for every pioneer family within a stone's throw of a maple tree.

In the southernmost reaches of Canada, maple syrup season can come as early as late February, but for most of us, the fun starts in mid-March or later. Like a cue to venture outdoors after a dull, cold winter, trees are ripe for tapping when the sun shines brightly in the late winter sky by day and temperatures drop below freezing at night. The warmth of the sun triggers the sap, which has been stored in the roots all winter, to rise up toward the branches, while at night, it retreats back towards the roots. Tapping siphons off a measure of the rising sap; fortunately, the tree doesn't suffer if the trunk is large enough.

When I got home from Alabama, I sent each of my southern friends a jar of my stuff. Never was I more proud of something I had made myself, and never did I consider myself more fortunate to live up here in the land of ice, snow and sugaring off.

Eight Sweet Steps to Maple Magic

Choose a Tree

(Tapping time is from mid-March to mid-April when days are bright, sunny and above freezing, and nights are crisp and below freezing.)

A hobby tapper can probably secure enough sap to make syrup from as few as three maples. Do not tap any tree smaller than 38 inches (96 cm) in circumference. Use only one tap per tree unless the tree is much larger, that is at least 57 inches (144 cm) around. Two taps per tree is the limit to ensure that sugaring does not damage the tree. As a rule-of-thumb, each tap will yield 10 gallons (38 l) of sap throughout an approximate six-week season, producing 2 pints (1 l) of maple syrup.

STEP 1

Drill a Hole

At about chest height, drill a hole into the south (sunny) side of the tree, where the sap flows most freely. Use a 7/16″ bit (this size fits a standard spile). Drill on an upward angle. To protect the inner wood from disease or insect infestation, don't penetrate the trunk more than 3 inches.

STEP 2

Set the Spile

Tap the spile into place with a rubber mallet. Be sure to align it trough-down. If it's a bright sunny day, the sap will start running almost immediately.

STEP 3

Secure the Lid

Like threading a needle, drive the hinge rod through the lid and through the hole in the spile.

STEP 4

Secure the Bucket

Hang the bucket on the spile and let the lid fall into place on top.

The lid deflects bugs and other debris. Check the tap daily: On crisp, sunny days, it will be full to overflowing; on overcast days, the sap may not run at all.

STEP 5

Start the Boil

Collect enough sap to fill a cauldron and bring to a boil. Purists prefer to reduce their sap over an open wood fire, but a propane-powered corn-roast burner is much more convenient for small batches.

STEP 6

The Boil Continues

It will take several long hours, but as the sap reduces, it starts to turn an amber colour. As it steams, you'll notice that unmistakable aroma.

STEP 7

The Boil Continues Some More

As the sap boils further, the process might start to get tedious, but this is the stage that requires your keen attention. As the sap becomes thicker and perhaps darker, be careful not to let it burn. It is perhaps easier to drain off the sap at this stage and do some fine-tuning indoors on the stove. When the syrup reaches the right colour and consistency, it's ready for bottling. Strain it through a cheesecloth filter as you pour into bottles.

DAN NEEDLES

The Visiting Season

True confessions from the Ninth Concession

For three months every year, Nottawasaga Township is like the south of France. A breeze off Georgian Bay freshens the air and sheep frolic upon the green pastures. However, for the rest of the year, it's like Nottawasaga Township. Struggling through seven months of the Great Canadian Dark in this part of the country requires more than a good recipe for bean soup and a couple of hotel weekends in the city. For a family of six operating on a writer's income computed in declining Canadian dollars, the idea of a white sand beach in April must remain pretty much a pipe dream.

After ten winters out here on the farm, I have found that the key to mental health in heavy frost and low light is to maintain a sense of purpose and to seek out human community. Of course, this is not a novel idea. Social life in the countryside was originally organized around exactly this theme. Winter was the traditional visiting time, when roads were snow-packed and easier to travel, and the work around the farm was lighter. Today, the old farm population has all but disappeared, but many of the organizations they left behind still survive.

Here in Nottawasaga, we tend to lean on two of the oldest institutions for relief: the Duntroon Anglican Church and the Collingwood Fair Board. We have also invented a new one: the Dallas Sideroad Literary Society. Membership in these three groups guarantees that you are never more than 48 hours away from a potluck supper. Together, they serve as the emotional equivalent of a tanning bed.

Last year, the church held several suppers, a theatre excursion and a dozen planning sessions for the renovation of a schoolhouse for our new couples club and Sunday school. Right now, we're up at the hall with crowbars and paint brushes doing the work and planning a big fund-raising dinner themed around the last dinner on the Titanic.

The fair board meets relentlessly all winter in regular monthly sessions as an executive, in committees, as work parties, most often with food, even if it's only a box of donuts and a coffee perk. The fall fair is still six months off, but we exhaust ourselves in debate, decision making and storytelling far into the night.

The literary society has no membership dues, no agenda and no constitution. Club meetings occur spontaneously, by invitation only and are held around a large antique billiard table. There is only one rule and it is a firm one: any member who brings a book to the meeting will have his cue privileges retired.

In these months of low cumulus and long icicles, a lot of good work is done by citizens with a strong instinct for public service and their own diversion. There is one community I know of, about an hour southwest of us, that holds at least one dance in aid of fire victims every year. Last winter, it came time for the dance but there were no fires, so they had to go out and burn down a small shed to give the evening official standing. In the town of Rockwood, I know some manic farmers who take pause from playing elaborate practical jokes on each other to hold a "March blahs" dance for the community. Hundreds turn out to see them tell awful jokes in a joke booth, sing songs and put on macabre displays of line dancing. The place is always packed and proceeds got to local charities.

> The key to mental health in heavy frost and low light is to maintain a sense of purpose and to seek out human community.

Maybe by the time you read this, the sound of rushing water in the ditches will have signaled the end of the visiting season. That's when we will stumble outside, blinking like groundhogs in the bright sunshine, grateful to these groups for our mental health, and ready to face a growing season full of promise.

A Taste of Winter

by Darlene King

Chocolate Truffles

THESE LITTLE chunks of indulgence dissolve on the tongue, surrendering an exquisite explosion of flavour. They have double the chocolate taste: part bittersweet, part sweet milk-chocolate. Not to be missed.

MAKES APPROXIMATELY 24 PIECES

8 oz	bittersweet chocolate, chopped	225 g
⅔ cup	whipping cream	160 ml
2 Tbsp	butter	30 ml
COATING		
½ cup	cocoa powder	120 ml

Put the chopped chocolate in a medium-sized, heat-proof bowl and set aside.

Place the cream and butter in a small saucepan and gently bring to a boil. Remove from heat and pour the mixture over the chocolate pieces. Using a rubber spatula, mix until the chocolate has melted.

(Option: To flavour the centres, add 4 tbsp of your favourite liqueur at this point.)

Cover and place in the freezer until thickened and set, approximately 2 hours. When firm enough to handle, scoop the mixture and roll between your hands into balls. Make them smooth and uniform in size. Place the chocolate balls on a cookie sheet lined with baking parchment and return them to the freezer to firm up again.

COATING

To coat the truffles, roll each truffle in the cocoa powder. Place the coated truffles back on the tray and refrigerate to harden.

Arrange the hardened truffles in candy cups and store in the freezer until ready to serve. Truffles can also be stored in an airtight container. They will keep in the refrigerator for up to a week and in the freezer up to 3 months.

Hazelnut Chocolate Chunk Cookies

MAKES ABOUT 30 TO 35 LARGE COOKIES

21.5 oz	1 box fudge brownie mix	
½ cup	water	120 ml
⅓ cup	vegetable oil	80 ml
1	large egg	1
3 Tbsp	flour	45 ml
9 oz	bittersweet or milk chocolate, coarsely chopped	255 g
1½ cups	roasted hazelnuts, skins removed and coarsely chopped	360 ml

NUTS ARE a natural for Yuletide cookie recipes. This one calls for hazelnuts, a mainstay in festive cookery. The skins are a little tedious to remove, but the effort is rewarded with a cookie rich in nutty texture. But the crowning glory is, perhaps, the taste of generous chunks of chocolate.

Position a rack in the centre of the oven and preheat to 350°F (175°C). Spread the nuts in a single layer on a baking sheet and roast for 12 to 15 minutes, shaking the pan two or three times, until the nuts are golden beneath their skins. Wrap the nuts in a clean towel. When cool, the skins can be removed simply by rubbing the nuts back and forth inside the towel.

In a medium bowl, use a wooden spoon to stir together the brownie mix, water, oil, egg and flour. Fold in all except ¼ cup (60 ml) of the chocolate and ¼ cup (60 ml) of the hazelnuts. Drop the cookie dough on to a prepared baking sheet, one rounded tablespoon at a time, leaving at least 1 inch between cookies. Garnish the top of each cookie with several pieces of the reserved hazelnut and chocolate.

Line a baking sheet with aluminum foil. With the rack still in the centre of the oven and the heat still at 350°F (175°C), bake the cookies for 13 to 15 minutes, or until your fingertip leaves a slight indentation. Transfer the cookies to a wire rack and cool completely.

White and Dark Chocolate Almond Bark

MAKES 2 POUNDS (1 KG)

3 cups	almonds, lightly toasted	720 ml
6 oz	white chocolate, roughly chopped	170 g
12 oz	semi-sweet chocolate, roughly chopped	240 g

ALMOND BARK is one of those indulgences we allow ourselves at this time of year. Our variation produces nicely white and semi-sweet dark chocolate.

Preheat the oven to 350°F (170°C).

Choose a baking sheet with sides. Line it with baking parchment and set aside.

Toast the almonds on a second baking sheet for approximately 8 minutes or until just lightly browned, stirring occasionally. Remove from the oven and transfer to a large bowl to cool. Set aside.

Bring 1 inch (2.5 cm) of water to a simmer in the bottom of a double boiler. Melt the white chocolate in the top of the double boiler. Stir until completely melted. Remove from heat and set aside.

Melt the semi-sweet chocolate in the same manner. Remove from heat when completely melted. Stir in the toasted almonds, making sure all the nuts are coated. Pour the chocolate-nut mixture onto the lined baking sheet, using a spatula to spread evenly.

Spoon or drizzle the white chocolate over the dark. Drag a fork or a knife through the mixture to create a pattern, but do not blend too much or the marbled effect will be lost.

Cool at room temperature for 1 hour. Cover with plastic wrap and refrigerate until the bark firms up. Remove from the fridge and cut into irregular shapes. Refrigerate in a tightly sealed container until ready to serve.

Apple Cinnamon Coffee Cake

SERVES 10 TO 12

4	medium apples, peeled and diced	4
⅓ cup	granulated sugar	80 ml
2 tsp	ground cinnamon	10 ml
3 cups	all-purpose flour	720 ml
2½ cups	granulated white sugar	600 ml
1 Tbsp	baking powder	15 ml
1 tsp	ground cinnamon	5 ml
½ tsp	salt	2.5 ml
1 cup	vegetable oil	240 ml
4	large eggs, lightly beaten	4
½ cup	cold coffee	120 ml
½ cup	milk	120 ml
2½ tsp	vanilla extract	12.5 ml

GLAZE

1 cup	light brown sugar	240 ml
½ cup	butter	120 ml
¼ cup	cream	60 ml
1 tsp	vanilla	5 ml

COFFEE CAKE is one of the old faithfuls in any cook's repertoire. This delicious version is even better served the next day. It can be enjoyed with or without the glaze.

Preheat the oven to 325°F (160°C). Spray a 10-cup/2.5-L Bundt pan with cooking spray.

Mix the apples, ⅓ cup sugar and cinnamon together in a bowl. Distribute the mixture over the bottom of the pan.

Mix the flour, 2½ cups of sugar, baking powder, cinnamon and salt in a large bowl. Make a well in the centre of the bowl and set aside.

In a separate bowl, mix together the vegetable oil, eggs, cold coffee, milk and vanilla extract.

When well combined, pour the mixture into the centre of the dry ingredients and stir. Pour the batter over the apple mixture. Bake for 1 hour or until a toothpick inserted into the centre comes out dry. Cool on a rack.

TO MAKE THE GLAZE

When the cake is completely cooled, bring the brown sugar, butter and cream to a boil in a small pot over medium-high heat, stirring constantly. Remove from the heat once the mixture just comes to a boil, and stir in the vanilla. Beat the glaze with a wooden spoon until it is cooled and thick enough to glaze the cake.

Hot Mulled Cider

SERVES 8

2 quarts	apple cider	2 l
4	4-inch (10 cm) cinnamon sticks	4
2	apples, stuffed with 3 cloves each	2
1	whole allspice berry	1

MULLED CIDER is a great way to beat the winter chills. The addition of clove-stuffed apples adds a punch of flavour.

Combine all the ingredients in a large pot and simmer for 30 minutes. Strain before serving.

Further Resources

A Straw Bale Homestead

For more information on building with straw see:

- Magwood, Chris. *More Straw Bale Building.* New Society Publishers: 2005.
- Steen, Athena. *The Straw Bale House.* Chelsea Green Publishing Co.: 1994.
- King, Bruce. *Buildings of Earth and Straw.* Ecological Design Press: 1997.

An Heirloom Garden

Seeds of Diversity, a seed exchange group that features heritage seeds, can be contacted at Box 36, Station Q, Toronto ON M4T 2L7 or at www.seeds.ca

Country Careers

Paul and Sarah Edwards, an American husband-and-wife team, write best-selling books that cover just about every aspect of the home business market. Another source is *Home Inc.: The Canadian Home-Based Business Guide* by Douglas and Diana Gray published by McGraw-Hill Ryerson in 1994. Good websites include The Canadian Telework Association (www.ivc.ca) and Small Biz Pro (www.smallbizpro.com).

Everybody Must Get Stones

The Dry Stone Wall Association of Canada is a good source for more information on this ancient building technique. www.dswac.ca

Eyes Wide Open

Briarcliffe Inn is located about 15 minutes from the Confederation Bridge a half hour west of Charlottetown. For more information, write Mary and Bill Kendrick at 274 Salutation Cove Road, RR #1, Bedeque, PEI C0B 1C0 or at www.briarcliffeinn.com

Heirlooms in the Barnyard

Rare Breeds Canada is actively recruiting rural dwellers, especially hobby farmers, interested in raising old breeds of livestock. For more information contact them at 1-341 Clarkson Rd., RR #1, Castleton, Ontario K0K 1M0 or at www.rarebreedscanada.ca

Ram-ifications

For more information on rammed earth construction see:
- Easton, David. *The Rammed Earth House*. Chelsea Green Publishing Co.: 1996.
- King, Bruce. *Buildings of Earth and Straw*. Ecological Design Press: 1997.

Meror Krayenhoff offers weekend seminars on Salt Spring Island. Participants learn the basics of the technique, tour several local rammed earth houses and even get to do a little on-site ramming. Check www.sirewall.com for dates, fees and more information.

The Un-Garden

Habitat gardening teaches gardeners about relationships between plants, animals and insects and how to re-establish and conserve natural lands and improve biodiversity. Philip Fry, founder of the Old Field Garden at Kemptville, Ontario, holds wildflower habitat gardening workshops in spring and fall and sells woodland plants from his nursery. www.oldfieldgarden.on.ca

Contributors

Grace Butland

Grace Butland is a freelance writer and fibre artist who lives the *Harrowsmith* dream in Parkers Cove, Nova Scotia. Avid gardeners, she and her husband grow and "put by" much of their annual food supply.

Tom Cruickshank

Tom Cruickshank has been *Harrowsmith*'s editor since 1997. He is the prototypical *Harrowsmith* reader, having gone from dreaming about country life to owning a small country house on 2 acres to a recent move to a rambling Victorian farmhouse on a 75-acre hobby farm near Port Hope, Ontario. Tom has found his niche growing vegetables and raising chickens. He has an abiding interest in heritage architecture and has written five books on the subject.

Amy Jo Ehman

Amy Jo Ehman has one foot in the city (Saskatoon) and one foot on the family farm in the big old catalogue house where she grew up. Her writing passions are food and rural life, her cooking passion is bread, and her gardening passion is zucchini (and anything that goes with this versatile vegetable). She has been reading *Harrowsmith Country Life* a lot longer than she has been writing for it so her country heart is warmed to be included in this anthology.

Tim Farquhar

Tim Farquhar is a renovator and cabinetmaker who lives on a 165-acre sheep farm near Ayton, Ontario. He is a frequent DIY contributor to *Harrowsmith*.

Carol Hall

Carol Hall, of Denman Island, British Columbia, has been gardening with a passion for almost four decades. She has written over 200 magazine articles, several of which have been reprinted in anthologies. Her own book *Gardening in the Pacific Northwest*, co-authored with her husband and gardening partner Norm Hall, will be released in early 2008.

Marc Huminilowycz

Marc Huminilowycz is a transplanted city dweller who lives and works out of his ecologically-friendly home overlooking Ontario's scenic Beaver Valley. In addition to writing for *Harrowsmith* and local publications, Marc and his wife Egle operate a busy marketing communications agency called Sideroad Communications Inc.

Darlene King

As the Food Editor for *Harrowsmith*, Darlene King has been tempting readers with delicious recipes since 1997. She's a Cordon-Bleu chef who has run her own gourmet shop, penned her own cookbook and presided over a dining room at a summer lodge in Ontario's cottage country. Darlene is keen on all country pursuits—from perennials to chickens to orchard fruit—and her latest venture is a foray into sheep husbandry.

Craille Maguire Gillies

Craille Maguire Gillies is an editor and freelance writer who writes about gardening, lifestyle and environmental topics. Her work has appeared in *The Globe and Mail*, *Canadian Geographic* and *enRoute*. She lives in Montreal, which she explores with her indefatigable golden retriever.

Kathryn McHolm

Kathryn McHolm is an artist and garden designer who lives and works in Port Hope, Ontario.

Dan Needles

Dan Needles is a long-time columnist for *Harrowsmith,* and is the author of the successful "Wingfield Farm" stage plays. He and his family live on a small farm near Georgian Bay.

John Shaw-Rimmington

After many years restoring historic stone and brick buildings, John now specializes in using stone in landscaping and building traditional dry stone walls. He is currently the president of the Dry Stone Wall Association of Canada and teaches courses in dry stone construction and structural stone garden design.

Bridget Wayland

Bridget Wayland is *Harrowsmith*'s Senior Editor. She considers this job her calling—her parents subscribed to the magazine and lived the *Harrowsmith* lifestyle. Bridget lives in a country farmhouse in Quebec's Eastern Townships where she practices her organic gardening skills.

Karyn Woodland

Karyn Woodland is a freelance writer, yoga teacher and flower gardener who lives, works, and plays in rural Metchosin, near Victoria, British Columbia. She shares a home (and a huge garden) with husband Joel, daughter Camas, and their lively Lhasa Apso/Terrier cross Daisy.

List of Articles

FOLLOWING IS A list of the articles contained in this book and the *Harrowsmith Country Life* issues in which they were first published:

Spring

EVERY HOME SHOULD HAVE ONE, by Tom Cruickshank was first published in the June 2002 issue.

BOXES FOR THE BIRDS, by Tim Farquhar, was first published in the June 2003 issue.

THE UN-GARDEN, by Craillie Maguire Gilles, was first published in the April 2002 issue.

COUNTRY DREAMING, a *Harrowsmith Country Life* Staff Report, was first published as *Say Goodbye to the City* in the October 2002 issue.

HOMESTEAD SWEET HOMESTEAD, by Bridget Wayland, was first published in the June 2000 issue.

PLOTTING WITH MOTHER NATURE, by Carol Hall, was first published in the August 2005 issue.

A PUBLIC LIFE: TRUE CONFESSIONS FROM THE NINTH CONCESSION, by Dan Needles, was first published in the June 2005 issue.

SHARE AND SHARE ALIKE, by Grace Butland, was first published in the April 2001 issue.

A TASTE OF SPRING, by Darlene King
· Cream of Asparagus Soup was first published in the June 1999 issue.
· Maple Shortbread Cookies was first published in the December 1998 issue.
· Rhubarb Sour Cream Pie was first published in the April 2002 issue.

· Spinach Salad with Warm Bacon and Maple Walnut Dressing was first published in the April 2001 issue.

Summer

EYES WIDE OPEN, by Tom Cruickshank, was first published in the August 2004 issue.

LOVE AMONG THE RUINS, a *Harrowsmith Country Life* Staff Report, was first published in the June 1998 issue.

IF YOU CAN'T STAND THE HEAT, GET OUT OF THE KITCHEN, by Kathryn McHolm, was first published in the August 2004 issue.

AN HEIRLOOM GARDEN, by Tom Cruickshank, was first published in the June 2001 issue.

MAIL ORDER MANORS, by Amy Jo Ehman, was first published in the June 2005 issue.

VIVA VERANDAHS!, by Tom Cruickshank, was first published in the August 2002 issue.

CATCH A FALLING STAR, by Marc Huminilowycz, was first published in the August 2005 issue.

THE SLOW FOOD CHAIN: TRUE CONFESSIONS FROM THE NINTH CONCESSION, by Dan Needles, was first published in the October 2006 issue.

A TASTE OF SUMMER, by Darlene King
· Oriental Chicken Kebabs with Pineapple and Mango was first published in the June 1999 issue.
· Pancetta, Pecan and Sun-dried Tomato Pasta was first published in the August 2002 issue.

· Sesame Roasted Broccoli & Green Beans was first published in the August 2006 issue.
· Tomato Bruschetta, Three Ways was first published in the August 2002 issue.

Autumn

A STRAW BALE HOMESTEAD, by Tom Cruickshank, was first published in the October 2002 issue.

BEAUTY AND THE BEASTS, by Dan Needles, was first published in the October 1999 issue.

BEST IN SHOW, by Tom Cruickshank, was first published in the October 1998 issue.

GOODBYE CITY LIFE!, by Tom Cruickshank, was first published in the October, 2005 issue.

A DOG'S LIFE, by Karyn Woodland, was first published in the October 2002 issue.

TOMATOES FOR TOMORROW, by Darlene King, was first published in the October 2001 issue.

COUNTRY ETIQUETTE: TRUE CONFESSIONS FROM THE NINTH CONCESSION, by Dan Needles, was first published in the August 1999 issue.

A TASTE OF AUTUMN, by Darlene King
· Apple Cranberry Pie with Oatmeal Walnut Topping was first published in the December 1997 issue.
· Butternut Squash Pasta with Zucchini and Lemon was first published in the October 1999 issue.
· Medley of Three Squash Soup was first published in the October 1999 issue.

Winter

RAM-IFICATIONS, by Tom Cruickshank, was first published in the June 2005 issue.

EVERYBODY MUST GET STONES, by John Shaw-Rimmington, was first published in the August 2005 issue.

COUNTRY CAREERS, by Bridget Wayland, was first published in the December 2000 issue.

VEGETABLES BY DESIGN, by Bridget Wayland, was first published in the April 2003 issue.

HEIRLOOMS IN THE BARNYARD, a *Harrowsmith Country Life* Staff Report, was first published in the October 2004 issue.

TAPPING WINTER'S SWEET BOUNTY, a *Harrowsmith Country Life* Staff Report, was first published as *The Sweet Treat of Spring* in the February 2004 issue.

THE VISITING SEASON: TRUE CONFESSIONS FROM THE NINTH CONCESSION, by Dan Needles, was first published as *The Visiting Season is Almost Over* in the April 1998 issue.

A TASTE OF WINTER, by Darlene King
· Apple Cinnamon Coffee Cake was first published in the October 2005 issue.
· Chocolate Truffles was first published in the December 2000 issue
· Hazelnut Chocolate Chunk Cookies was first published in the December 1998 issue.
· Hot Mulled Cider was first published in the December 2003 issue
· White and Dark Chocolate Almond Bark was first published in the December 2002 issue.

Index

Picture Credits

Photographs

Front cover: Yvonne Duivenvoorden; back cover Wayne Barrett (top), Vern McGrath (bottom)

Peter Anderson © Dorling Kindersley: p. 52; Wayne Barrett: p. 79, p. 80, p. 82, p. 84, p. 87, p. 226, p. 230; Jeffrey Bodset: pp. 188–199; Demetrio Carrasco © Dorling Kindersley: p. 69; Carroll and Carroll: p. 152, pp. 154–156, p.158; Chris Cheadle: pp. 172–175; Chris Cheadle/Getty Images: p. 10; John deVisser: p. 124, p. 126 (top), p. 127, p. 128; Terence Dickenson: p. 130; Dorling Kindersley: p. 71; Yvonne Duivenvoorden: p. 164, p. 167, p. 169–171; Amy Jo Ehman: p. 120, p. 122; Turid Forsyth: p. 32, pp. 35–41, p. 46, pp. 61–62; Gavin Hellier/Getty Images: p. 136; Jacqui Hurst © Dorling Kindersley: p. 216; Alan Keohane © Dorling Kindersley: p. 236; Frans Lemmens/Getty Images: p. 184; Archie MacDonald: p. 50; Scott McAlpine: pp. 176–178; Robert McCaw: p. 24, p. 26 (vignette), p. 28 (vignette), p. 30 (vignette); Vern McGrath: p. 2, p. 14, pp. 17–20, pp. 26–31, p. 41, p. 88, pp. 90–91, p. 94; Ian O'Leary © Dorling Kindersley: p. 132, p. 180, p. 242; Pierre St. Jacques: p. 5, p. 74, p. 108, pp. 110–113, p. 116, p. 118; Jason Santerre: p. 228, p. 235; Mike Wallace: p. 97, pp. 99–105, p. 126 (bottom), p. 140, p. 143, p. 145–146, pp. 148–150; p. 200, pp. 203–207, p. 231, p. 233, pp. 239–240

Illustrations and Paintings

Normand Cousineau: p. 208; Nicola di Lauro: p. 22, p. 86, p. 150, p. 198; Pierre Durand: p. 34, p. 115, p. 168; Albert J. Clark, *Bramhope Romeo*, 1909/ Private Collection/Courtesy Canadian Museum of Animal Art: p. 162; John Sloan Gordon, *Martimas*, 1898/Private Collection/Courtesy Canadian Museum of Animal Art: p. 163; Edwin Frederick Holt, *A Flock of Sheep in a Barn*, 1887/Private Collection/Courtesy Canadian Museum of Animal Art: p. 160; Marc Mongeau: p. 54, p. 56, p. 48, p. 64, p. 219, p. 221, p. 223; Michel Poirier: p. 93, p. 192, p. 204; Western Development Museum: p. 121, p. 123; Richard Whitford, *A Prize Middle White Sow in a Field*, 1882/Iona Antiques, London: p. 161